CULTIVATING EMPATHY

CULTIVATING EMPATHY

The Worth and Dignity of Every Person—
Without Exception

Nathan C. Walker

Skinner House Books
Boston

www.skinnerhouse.org

www.CultivatingEmpathy.org

Printed in the United States

Cover design by Kathryn Sky-Peck
Cover photo by Neale Cousland/Shutterstock
Author photo by Vikram Paralkar
Text design by Suzanne Morgan

print ISBN: 978-1-55896-774-8
eBook ISBN: 978-1-55896-775-5

6 5 4 3 2 1
18 17 16

Library of Congress Cataloging-in-Publication Data

Names: Walker, Nathan C., 1975- author.
Title: Cultivating empathy : the worth and dignity of every person—without
    exception / Nathan C. Walker.
Description: Boston : Skinner House Books, 2016.
Identifiers: LCCN 2016001198 (print) | LCCN 2016005424 (ebook) | ISBN
    9781558967748 (pbk. : alk. paper) | ISBN 9781558967755 ()
Subjects: LCSH: Empathy. | Unitarian Universalist Association—Doctrines.
Classification: LCC BJ1475 .W34 2016 (print) | LCC BJ1475 (ebook) | DDC
    177/.7—dc23
LC record available at http://lccn.loc.gov/2016001198

I feel awkward writing a book titled *Cultivating Empathy* because I know that I have been profoundly flawed in my ability to be empathetic with others. I do not see the title as a proclamation of my abilities but rather a grand challenge for me to live a more compassionate life. I, therefore, dedicate this book to all the people I have harmed so that they know that I am using the experiments detailed here to accept this challenge and to cultivate my character.

That which dominates our
imaginations and our thoughts
will determine our lives, our character.

—RALPH WALDO EMERSON

CONTENTS

FOREWORD

I've always loved books of true-life adventure stories far more than books of theory, and I thank Nate Walker for creating the former rather than the latter. He brings us a collection of radically different moral dilemmas, which at first might seem unrelated. And then he names the ways that they are related, giving us an overarching framework to think about how we can react in seemingly intractable situations of our own.

The framework that Nate lifts up is the moral imagination. What a helpful way to think about what is and isn't happening, and to try to stumble forward, however challenging this route may prove to be! Nate draws upon the medical ethics curriculum from the University of Kansas, which defines the moral imagination as "the ability to anticipate or project oneself into the middle of a moral dilemma and understand all the points of view." Of course, none of us can ever do that completely. Often, we can barely understand or articulate our own point of view in a difficult moment. Yet, imperfect as we all are, I've seen people exhibit the same capacity that Nate describes in his own life. In fact, reading this book helped me to explain a situation I've puzzled over for more than thirty years.

Allow me to share an adventure of my own. The group Women Against Violence Against Women, in the Twin Cities of Minnesota, was strong and bold and fun. We held a successful Take Back the Night march in 1979, and then again in 1980. In 1981, many of us who had been early members of the group left, and the leadership floundered. That year, there was fighting. Deep, deep fighting, the kind where soul-scorching accusations were made using words like racism and homophobia, and each side felt wronged and hurt. Eventually it got so bad that the group announced that it was going to cancel the 1981 march and just shut down. Some of us who had since moved on from the organization came to an open meeting to talk together about what might be done.

We came into a room full of finger pointing and yelling and blame, now focused on where the money should go when the organization shut down. Into the middle of these factions—both sides might as well have been holding swords and shields and wearing armor—Sherri Menzer, a Quaker woman who had put her life into founding this organization but had since also moved on, spoke in a clear, quiet voice. I've always wished I could see this moment on film because when she spoke, something happened.

As near as I can remember, Sherri said something like this: "This organization was conceived in love, born in love, and it would break my heart if its life ended with acrimony and bitterness. I can see that those of us who left did so without sufficient care for those who came after us, and for that I am profoundly sorry. We did not do what we should have to pass the leadership on. I am so sorry that those of you who have been doing this work have suffered so much doing it, and that you have not experienced the love and joy that we did. I don't care where the money goes. I care about the spirit with which the money is passed on to whoever receives it, for that spirit is the legacy of this organization."

When I write that, it seems simple, almost obvious. It is impossible to know how such a simple statement could have dissolved what felt like cement walls in the room. In that moment, those words were like a magic key that unlocked the invisible gates and released all the prisoners. There were walls, and then we were in an open field, together. First there was sneering and disdainful interruption, eye-rolling and yelling, and then, suddenly, many of us—old and new members alike—had tears running down our faces. We became centered in our own longings for the group's well being and in our own imperfection, holding our grief about what had gone wrong.

After reading this book, I now have language to describe what I witnessed: Sherri Menzer's moral imagination allowed us all to see what we had been unable to see before—a place where shame turned to grief, accusations turned to unmet longings, and heart opened to heart.

What a gift it is, to have a conceptual framework into which to place that foundational, profound experience! Knowing what unlocked that door gives me hints about how other similar doors might open. It takes this experience out of the realm of an isolated and unrepeatable event and offers up the use of moral imagination as a gift, as a spiritual practice, to use in the conscious way that Nate Walker uses it in the life experiences he describes in this book.

I also appreciate how he shares his struggle to consistently use the moral imagination and talks openly about his failed attempts. He shows that using the moral imagination as a daily discipline is a challenge that cannot always be accepted or won, especially when our society is so divided about how to treat one another.

We live in polarized times, when rage and indifference toward people who are Muslim, transgender, black, brown, disabled, or otherwise deemed "dispensable" are propelling daily acts of violence and oppression. It is easy for each of us to feel helpless and insignificant, as if the choices we make do nothing to transform this landscape.

For instance, I wonder how we might use the moral imagination as a tool to move closer toward promoting a world in which Black and Brown Lives Matter. I wonder how the world would look different if those of us who are white, as I am, used the moral imagination as a spiritual practice to de-center our own experience and to pay deep, compassionate attention to the lived experiences of people of color. To believe and honor what we see and hear could help us realize that, no matter what other aspects of our lives are oppressive or debilitating, white privilege is always at work. This practice of de-centering ourselves, of putting the lives and needs of others before (or at least next to) our own, is familiar to us as parents or lovers. To engage in this practice is to be transformed, if we are white, which is terrifying, and means giving up a great deal. Only the moral imagination can reassure us that what we gain (connection, reality, wholeness) is much greater than what we lose (comfort, ignorance, disassociation).

The moral imagination might also transform how those of us who are white talk with our white neighbors. In many of my conversations with other white people, specifically white people who insist that we live in a post-racial society, I feel a profound "miss" in the center—as if I am talking with people who speak a different language. If I'm honest, perhaps I am terrified that I am not so fundamentally different from them, and so I close my heart instead of reaching into that place where we are missing each other. I write them off instead of presuming that they have something to teach me. What if I believed that when I silently judge them to differentiate them from me, I am losing some important insights? Instead I could exercise my moral imagination to see that we are both limited by the same dehumanizing belief systems. The moral imagination as a spiritual practice would have me insist that there is a meaningful place where we can connect, and that we will be stronger if we do.

Nate Walker has provided us with the gift of his own roadmap as he engages in a bold, risk-taking journey of following those two revolutionary words that open imagination and life: What if? I suspect that all of us who read this book have, consciously or unconsciously, engaged in similar moments of boldness, of the moral imagination. Reading these chapters, recognizing similar experiences that have already occurred in our own lives, can help us to recommit ourselves, intentionally and purposefully, to our own spiritual practice of the moral imagination.

Let's be real: We live in a time when many of the people with the cultural megaphones are not sharing imaginative stories of hope and possibility. If we are to continue as a people, it will be up to regular folks like us, individually and collectively, to find ways to create a more just, more compassionate way forward together. This book provided me deep and real support for that work, and I am deeply grateful to Nate Walker for writing it. I hope that it strengthens your own practice of moral imagination as well. The parched world is in need of the greening that such a practice brings.

—Meg Riley, senior minister, Church of the Larger Fellowship

INTRODUCTION

Over a period of several months in 1960 in New Orleans, child psychologist Robert Coles spoke with Ruby Bridges, a six-year-old African American who was threatened and taunted by people who opposed her enrollment in a segregated school.

She told Coles she felt sorry for the people who were trying to kill her.

He clarified, "You feel sorry for them?"

"Well, don't you think they need feeling sorry for?" she said.

Later, he wrote, "I sat there stunned. I was applying standard psychology, trying to help her realize that she was maybe angry at these people, and bitter and anxious, and she was telling me that she prayed for them. I was struck dumb and I was silent because I had to reflect upon this child's wisdom."

Coles spent his career listening to people's wisdom and sharing his own, writing more than sixty books. One of those books influenced my life—*The Call of Stories: Teaching and the Moral Imagination*. His writings taught me about the power of storytelling. Both fictional stories and true ones teach us that the human capacity to have empathy for another is not simply a creative impulse but a moral one.

His writings led me to study the variety of ways that people have used the term *moral imagination*. I particularly appreciate how doctors at the University of Kansas School of Medicine defined it as "the ability to anticipate or project oneself into the middle of a moral dilemma or conflict and understand all the points of view."

Understanding does not necessarily mean agreement. I may disagree with your point of view, but often my disagreement prevents me from understanding the true, untainted nature of your standpoint. If I never demonstrate that I understand you, then I cannot expect you to understand me. Understanding is a type of sympathetic awareness of another. Even more powerful is mutual understanding between two or more people—the fertile soil in which the moral imagination is planted and peace is grown. Our moral duty, therefore, is to till our understanding for one another and to plant our words and actions as the seeds of an ethical empathy. Failure to do so creates misperceptions and misunderstandings, which are the roots of conflict, stereotypes, and violence. The antidote to these aggressions is to cultivate mutual understanding, plant seeds of the moral imagination, and, hopefully, reap peaceful coexistence.

Some scholars suggest that Edmund Burke first used the term moral imagination in 1790 in *Reflections on the Revolution in France*. The idiom is neither a contemporary conception nor a scholarly one. Throughout the ages, communities and civilizations have employed the idea behind it, calling on people to treat others as they themselves want to be treated. The Golden Rule, of course, is one way to evoke moral empathy in one another.

In an interview, Coles once said, "Morality defines not only how we get along with the world and one another, and the rules of life; it characterizes our very nature. Morality has to do with human connection. It has to do with the kind of connection that responds to others, and in turn earns the caring response of others. If we are deprived of our morality, we're deprived of an essential part of ourselves."

Ruby Bridges invited Coles and, by extension, all of us, to imagine the torturous existence the segregationist white supremacist experienced when threatening her life. Empathy for a violent racist? This was not inconceivable for a six-year-old and her family. Ruby did not excuse this toxic behavior—she simply distinguished it from the person imprisoned by it. Nor did her caregivers tolerate such crude and violent acts. Rather, her family kept her safe while also teaching her to pray in the same way that they were taught, using Jesus' dying words: "Father, forgive them; for they do not know what they are doing" (Luke 23:34).

Christianity was a source of morality for the Bridges family. And yet those calling for the death of this six-year-old girl also considered themselves to be Christians and read the same scripture that the Bridges did. This contradiction illustrates that the imagination, like religion, has both a moral side that can inspire empathy and compassion and a shadow side that, as in this case, can breed systematic discrimination, hatred, and violence.

Barbaric acts are made possible when we "otherize" another person. In his book *Reconciliation: Mission and Ministry in a Changing Social Order,* Robert Schreiter classified seven ways of distinguishing "the other":

> We can *demonize* the other, treating the other as someone to be feared and eliminated if possible. We can, on the other hand, *romanticize* the other, treating the other as far superior to ourselves. We can *colonize* the other, treating the other as inferior. . . . We can *generalize* the other, treating the other as non-individual. . . . We can *trivialize* the other by ignoring what makes the other disturbingly different. We can *homogenize* the other by claiming that there really is no difference. We can *vaporize* the other by refusing to acknowledge the presence of the other at all.

Cultivating Empathy is, primarily, a collection of historical and contemporary accounts of the negative forms of otherizing—demonizing, colonizing, and so on. Some chapters, however, focus on how otherizing can also occur when we consciously or subconsciously project positive images onto people, romanticizing them. I have come to learn that whether we demonize or romanticize other people, we still *dehumanize* them—we *demoralize* them—while corrupting our own moral capacity. Our power to dehumanize, to demoralize others and ourselves, stems from our undisciplined, unprincipled minds.

A proven remedy for otherizing is to employ the moral imagination as an everyday spiritual practice. I use the term *spiritual* not to describe a supernatural or out-of-body experience. Rather, I mean the nonmaterial aspects of our moral and intellectual development. For me, that development is ultimately a religious challenge.

Building upon the ways humanities scholars have used the concept, as Robert Coles did in psychology, I have spent the last decade experimenting with how to integrate the moral imagination as a religious practice. I have been doing so by trying to use it as a spiritual discipline, as one would use other practices such as meditation or prayer, confession or fasting, worship or pilgrimage. I have employed the moral imagination as a religious discipline to inform my teaching and preaching, to enrich my internal life, and to tend to my relationships, especially with those with whom I am in conflict.

The most promising aspect of this humanistic discipline is that it is contagious. I have witnessed countless members of the Unitarian Universalist congregations that I have served as minister in New York and Philadelphia integrate the moral imagination into their own practices. When this happens, I feel like a teacher surpassed by a pupil in knowledge and skill. I am awed by these members' character, grateful for their courage, and inspired by them to continue the practice. In these moments, I have been known to grant congregants the title "personal spiritual trainer" in the middle of a worship service. I call out their names and publicly thank them for becoming my PSTs.

Personal spiritual trainers are people whose words and deeds are so profoundly grounded in ethical behavior that I cannot help but pause and admire the virtues in them that I seek to embody. One of the greatest privileges in my ministerial career has been looking out into the pews to witness a sea of my spiritual guides—

people whose everyday actions skillfully contributed to our community. Thanks to them, I felt as though I always had the best seat in the house.

The stories you are about to read took place in New York City and Philadelphia, where I was a Director of Religious Education at the Fourth Universalist Society from 2002 to 2004; a seminarian at Union Theological Seminary from 2002 to 2005; a ministerial intern at the Unitarian Church of White Plains from 2005 to 2006; a consulting minister at the Unitarian Church of Staten Island from 2006 to 2007; and as a senior minister at the First Unitarian Church of Philadelphia from 2007 to 2014.

Time and time again, PSTs have modeled for me and for fellow congregants how to successfully experiment with the moral imagination. When they do, something remarkable happens. The gathered community becomes a training ground where we learn not only how to be *first responders* to oppressive agendas but where we practice how to become ethical *agenda setters*.

We set these moral agendas when we come to community to lay down our moral failures. We all need a place where we can admit and reflect upon our unfulfilled virtues while being cared for and simultaneously being held to some higher standard. I need others to learn and grow. I need a community to help me imagine another way of being in the world. I do not need to be shamed, or pounded with dogma, or wounded with creeds. Many people came to the congregations I served in New York and Philadelphia seeking the same refuge—a shame-free zone. For these reasons, my PSTs and I were compatible co-religionists who sought to live with intentionality and grow in our spiritual maturity.

My PSTs have kept me from irresponsibly living in the shadow side of my imagination, where I once mastered the skill of brooding over conflicts, rehearsing my role as both the victim and hero in all my stories. My PSTs taught me to first observe these thought patterns, then to challenge myself to accurately recount conflicts rather than retelling them with the sole intent of justifying my actions, at the cost of demeaning and trivializing

XXII ❖ CULTIVATING EMPATHY

those with whom I was in conflict. Ultimately, these exercises forced me to mourn the loss of many years of my life in which I had trained myself to privilege gossip over reality, treating every opinion I had as if it were a verifiable truth. I am grateful to my community for saving me from spending a lifetime living as if my opinions were facts.

From the shadows in my character, I began to see a new reality, a new way of being. Rather than being defensive, I began to be curious. I started to ask, Why am I behaving in these ways? When and where did I learn these patterns? Why did I react in this way, and would others have done the same? What was it about that person's language or behavior that had so much power over me? What was keeping me from cultivating genuine empathy for those I previously held in contempt? Was it my pride? Was it my fierce need to be right? At what cost? The cost of eroding the humanity of another while diminishing my own?

My PSTs taught me that the antidote to this circle of suffering was to begin a daily, lifelong experiment with the moral imagination. To *experiment* meant trying and trying again, aware that in some instances we succeed in being moral and in others we fail. *Imagination* meant intentionally envisioning something that is not apparent. It became a grand challenge to try and manifest these experiments in my everyday actions. I had to start by treating the moral imagination as a hypothesis that I would test—a vision that I would try to manifest. I began by conducting research on my words and actions and by observing the impact my choices had on others and myself. When I discovered positive, healthy results, I turned to my community to try to replicate my findings. Over time, I had to understand the changing variables that influenced my mixed results, all in pursuit of embodying the moral imagination.

These questions, these everyday experiments, required that I consciously visualize myself playing characters within a particular scene. Zen masters have similarly challenged practitioners to watch the drama of their lives without playing a lead role in it. By watching the drama, I differentiated between the role I was playing and the person I wanted to be in those situations. *Cultivating Empathy* documents some of these mundane squabbles and extraordinary clashes.

❖ ❖ ❖

I hope that the sometimes painful dramas in this book will inspire you, as readers, to refuse to be passive observers. I mean to capture your imagination by inviting you to picture yourself in similar situations and to experiment with different ways to resolve disputes.

In the first chapter, for instance, I recount the time I became angry with wealthy patrons of a theater who felt justified in taking my partner's seat, removing his coat from it and putting it on the ground while saying, "We sponsored this event." I have asked various youth groups to reenact this conflict. It is not surprising that they liked playing the parts of the "one-percenters," but they mostly loved mocking the minister (ahem, me) who publicly humiliated the woman in pearls by asking, "Are you famous? If not, let me help you be" while taking her photo.

My gross behavior serves as the first of several examples of failures in my moral imagination. I found that this encounter is helpful when introducing the subject of this book because the word "moral" can put people on the defensive. People have said to clergy throughout history, "Don't call me immoral. You are the hypocrite." That is the precise point here. I am a hypocrite.

By owning this damning title, I take responsibility for my moral failures and turn to my community for help. I need others to teach me how to be kind and empathetic. And, like a child who has not learned to speak, I need others to help identify my unmet needs and help me communicate. In this way, the minister is not the sole deliverer of morality; rather, he or she is one of many who is transformed by a community that teaches its members how to experiment with the moral imagination as an everyday spiritual discipline.

This book is my attempt at documenting my experiments with the moral imagination, from meeting my biological father for the first time; to witnessing a man die on an airplane; to corresponding with Pat Robertson's senior executive about homosexuality and the Bible; to mediating a conflict with skinheads, a punk band, and Homeland Security; and to meeting with leaders of Monsanto to discuss the ethics of genetically modified foods.

I hope that the encounters described in this book will inspire other individuals and communities to experiment with the moral imagination as well. This is urgent and necessary work because none of us are exempt from the shadow side of the imagination. At some point, we have all cast someone in our dramas in uncharitable ways. We have allowed our biases to justify escalating conflicts. We have allowed ourselves to erode the humanity of those we perceived to be our enemies while tarnishing our own character. Therefore, the moral imagination requires intentional discipline. This practice is a spiritual discipline because it involves examining the nonmaterial aspects of living a virtuous life. And it is a religious response because an intentional community helps to reinforce this new way of creating the moral fabrics that will hold all of us, without exception, in care.

The grand challenge of the moral imagination is an experiment that you are about to begin by placing yourself in my stories. These encounters are but a few of my experiments with living intentionally.

MEETING THE ONE PERCENT

We, as one strong body, are required to lead by being. When we feel the impulse to be the interrogator, we must choose to be the generator of visions larger than ourselves. When we feel the impulse to be enraged, we must accept the invitation to be empathetic and no longer make people the object of our aggression. When we feel the impulse to be furious, let us dare to be curious. When we feel the impulse to be righteous, let us transform our soapbox into a music box. Let us dare to be powerfully playful.

Sounds lovely, doesn't it? I shared these words with my congregation in Philadelphia one Sunday. And then . . . Tuesday rolled around.

❖   ❖   ❖

I was in New York City to meet my partner for a lecture at New York University. Vikram was really into this lecture series, which asks, "Would the world be better off without religion?" So when he asked whether I wanted to join him—a funny question to ask a minister—I said in a patronizing voice, "Yes, dear."

We arrived an hour and a half early because it was open seating, and were pleased to get the center two seats of the fifth row. Vikram was so excited, acting like a little kid, asking, Do you know about this speaker, and that idea, and this and that? He was adorable.

Just before the event started, I received a notification on my phone that Mayor Bloomberg had just evicted the Occupy Wall Street protesters. I started to complain about how this violated their First Amendment rights to assemble and petition, and then Vikram said he wanted to use the restroom before the event started. He put his coat on his seat and left, while I read about Yetta Kurland, one of the lawyers for the protesters, saying, "Win, lose, or draw, the 99 percent will continue to show up, continue to express themselves."

A little while later the usher announced, "Any empty seats can go to those who haven't yet found one." I told her that my partner was in the bathroom. She said, "Yeah, that's okay," and went to assist other people.

Then a woman came and picked up Vikram's coat from the seat next to me. I said, "I'm sorry, that's reserved. He's in the bathroom." She sat down anyway and the man with her, maybe her husband, sat down in the empty seat on the other side.

I said, "I'm sorry, my partner's in the bathroom. This seat is taken."

She remained seated, not saying anything. She stared straight ahead, as if pretending not to hear me, and passed Vikram's coat to the man she was with.

I started to explain again, "I'm sorry, but we have been here for over an hour and a half. We came all the way from Philadelphia." Just then, Vikram started to walk down the aisle. I said, "Look, he's right there."

She replied—and this is where it gets a little crazy. She said, "We sponsored this event."

Okay.

So, remember Sunday? Yeah. I said these words then: "When we feel the impulse to be enraged, we must accept the invitation to be empathetic and no longer make people the object of our aggression."

Well. I did not do that at all. Instead, I said, "Oh. *You're* the one percent. I've been wanting to meet you."

I continued, "You say you sponsored this event. Do you own the chair or the whole theater?"

It gets worse. From the aisle, Vikram asked, "Where's my coat?" I looked over to see that the man had put it on the floor. Thankfully, the people sitting next to the man picked it up and passed it to Vikram.

I stood and said, "She's a one-percenter—she thinks she owns the joint." People started to look at us. The woman's spine became erect, which seemed to add an extra glimmer to her pearls. I, well—I kept going. I said, "You must be someone really important. Are you famous? If not, let me help you be."

I took out my phone and started, yes, taking her photo. I said, "I think people should know how you behave in the public square." I pressed the little camera icon while saying, "I'll label this one *Entitlement.*"

Oh, my god. I cannot believe I behaved this way.

The lights started going down, and Vikram was already at another seat in the back of the theater. I picked up my things and went to the lobby to speak with the house manager to recount the incident. I said, "I want to show you this picture. I'm not going to do anything with it. I just want you to know how your sponsor is treating other patrons." The house manager was very apologetic and responded by offering us season passes to the lecture series. The irony was simply divine.

I returned to the theater, found a seat in the balcony, and enjoyed the talk. That is the end of the drama and the continuation of a completely different journey—the journey into the heart of the moral imagination.

❖ ❖ ❖

I shared what happened with a member of our congregation, Ranwa Hammamy. She was heading off to seminary and had a vibrant ministry in our community. I showed her the picture and, while giggling, said, "Look at her face. And look at those behind her, gasping with fear."

Ranwa paused, then asked me a powerful, spiritually mature question: "Nate, why are you keeping the picture?"

I paused, then answered her honestly: "Maybe it's pride. I feel wronged and want to gloat over putting her in her place." Her question gave me the opportunity to reflect.

I have come to realize that inside of me is a deep-rooted score-card on which I get points for humiliating people in the name of doing justice. Despite what I had said on Sunday, on Tuesday it was as though a circus ringmaster was calling out, "Step on up, boy, you just got a point for being *witty*. Yes. There you go; and here's another for being *sarcastic*. Ding, ding, ding. You showed her."

By many standards my do-justice card was chock full of points. But here is the thing—that is not my scorecard. My true scorecard is up there, on the pulpit with that Sunday reading—words that I wrote as a call to use the moral imagination as an everyday spiritu-al practice. This true scorecard is made possible each time people gather to remember why we do justice work in the first place.

I have to be honest. It is really hard for me to earn those kinds of Sunday points when living a Tuesday kind of life. I am here one day and there another day. I am in the struggle. I am in the struggle for an integrated life, where ideally my public words match my pri-vate deeds, where ideally my private thoughts mirror my deepest ideals, but where realistically neither is true.

The truth is, my impulses do not always spring from kindness. I have been trained to think that kindness is weak. I have been trained to believe that interrogation should be harsh and that rage is always justified. I have been trained to believe that justice looks like a mob of angry protesters storming the castle, screaming, "PEACE!"

All that does is make a lot of smoke and ash. Besides, scream-ing makes my face hurt.

I feel sad and a bit embarrassed to admit it, but it is true. I do not like that part of myself. I do not want to be known for humiliating people. I do not feel good when treating others this way. I regret the way I treated the woman in pearls and I use this book to formally express my apology to her.

It was certainly not the first time something like that has happened, and it will not be the last. After all, I am a liberal. I know how to spar with someone—especially during church committee meetings.

Why is it so easy for me to become what I set out against? The minute we see some injustice, we pounce. I am sorry, I mean to say, "I pounce." I cast myself in the role of the Righteous One. I have long since mastered this role. I rehearse it when watching the political pundit, when reading the flaming blog: It is the same old game, in which "success" is built upon demeaning others rather than making meaning of our lives.

How could I have made meaning in this situation? What were my options? To just give her the seat? To quietly sit by and smile nice and talk pretty? I am sharing this story not because there is some scripted answer. I am curious about what others would have done in this struggle. I want others to show me, coach me in a new way of playing the justice game. I want to be coached in exercising the options that were available to me at the time, in order to better know what options are available to me now.

Here is one alternative. Ranwa's question helped me play a different game. I began by deleting the picture. That was a good first step. Symbolically, I began to let go of a painful memory. Practically, I had one less tool to reinforce my tendency to brood.

I cannot help but wonder how other people picture the woman in pearls. Would they empathize with me more if she was a white woman in her early fifties who seemed to have had a facelift and whose blond hair was tightly sculpted?

What if she was an African-American woman in her early eighties who walked with a cane, whose distinguished grey hair and deep rich voice made her resemble Maya Angelou? In this scene, would you have more empathy for her than for me—a white male in his mid-thirties?

Does it matter what she looked like? It did for me in that particular moment. Her blond hair, pearls, tight white face, and erect spine tapped into my negative stereotype of the so-called one-percenters. "Those people" are not just wealthy, they are grossly privileged. They feel entitled and ready to evict anyone who gets in their way. I have spent years subconsciously using my imagination to typecast people in these roles, played out in the dramas of my mind, the dramas in which I play only the hero.

By keeping the photo of the white woman in pearls, by looking at it and sharing it with others, I reinforced my deeply embedded stereotypes. I used my imagination to demean her over and over again. I used the image to justify myself to others, reinforcing my self-cast role as the hero. Said another way, I first experienced a failure in the moral imagination in the way I treated her. I then multiplied that failure each time I treated the photo as evidence for her conviction.

This pattern became the poison that I unintentionally asked others to drink with me. It was as if I wanted others to join me in holding her in contempt and to empathize with me, the one who was wronged, the one who was justified in putting her in her place. In doing so, I used the photo as an invitation for others to join me in basking in the shadow side of the imagination—to join me in a significant failure of the moral imagination.

It took a self-differentiated person to disrupt this mirage. Ranwa did so with seven words: "Nate, why are you keeping the picture?" With this question the red velvet curtain fell and the house lights rose to reveal that no one was seated in the theater of my mind. There was no imagined audience cheering, "Encore!"

Rather than hearing applause I heard more questions. *Why did you treat her that way? Why are you using this photo as a trophy? Why do you want others to affirm your humiliating tactics?* These thoughts flowed because a fellow co-religionist kindly illuminated a new way.

I am deeply grateful to Ranwa for inspiring me to delete the photo. In that moment she served as my personal spiritual trainer, an ethical guide, reminding me of another way of being in the world. That is what healthy communities do for people, week after week. Ultimately, that is how I have come to define being religious today. We come to community to call one another back into a new kind of game, one that grants fulfilling ethical rewards.

You may be amused to know that months later, my friends were looking at photos on my phone when they found the one of the woman from the theater. I could not believe it. I should have known! After you delete a photo, you have got to *take out the trash.*

Life is like that. The things we thought we deleted are not completely erased. Only after we take that second step are we really free from becoming what we set out against. We take that second step when we return to our spiritual home to experience a new way of being.

Here is another passage from the words I shared during that worship service. It is humbling to know that I composed these words on Sunday, only to fail to embody them two days later.

What does justice-making look like, feel like, when we receive hostile communication? Are we hostile in return? Or is something else required of us? What we choose to do is a reflection of who we believe ourselves to be. It all depends on our beliefs about power.

I once believed that it was powerful to condemn wrongdoers. I believed it right to tear down another's unexamined assumptions and to vaporize those whose presence was not worthy of my attention. I believed that others were the cause of my aggression, others were to blame for my feelings of despair, disappointment, and righteous indignation.

Rather than anger serving as a signal that something was wrong, anger became the solution to all my problems. It felt good to fuel the addiction of righteousness. I was doing justice—I was doing justice—all while being an ass.

I have spent far too much energy using the public forum as a battlefield. I have spent far too much energy using the public forum to annihilate those I perceived to be my enemy. I have armed myself with faithful friends, so that each time we walked into a room, those present would shade their gaze and whisper in dread, "The liberals have arrived."

I used to believe that being feared was powerful. I used to believe it was my duty to free the oppressed. But when I react with righteous anger, I become the oppressor.

As Thích Nhất Hạnh, a Zen Buddhist, once said, "I came to set the prisoner free only to realize the prisoner was me."

❖ ❖ ❖

I begin this book on the moral imagination with my encounter with the woman in pearls because I want to pose a question to all justice-seeking friends. I am curious about the true nature of those who have dedicated their lives to human rights, to civil rights, to environmental justice: What makes us uniquely poised to be an effective, justice-seeking people? That is, what makes a liberal religious movement distinct from the Occupy Movement or the Freedom to Marry campaign or Amnesty International or any number of other justice groups? What is the purpose of being religious if we train one another to be asses in the public square? What tools do we collectively employ to keep us from causing others harm? When we teach one another to use the moral imagination effectively, are we poised to do something uniquely different than what the Sierra Club does, or the United Nations, or the World Bank? What is the true kernel of our religious community's justice work? Perhaps it is cultivating an ethical empathy for another, otherwise known as the moral imagination.

We have witnessed compassion manifested in the mindful approach of engaged Buddhists. Their very presence makes us pause and say with a deep exhale, "Oh, good, the Buddhists have arrived." We have witnessed a similar quality when Quakers enter a room and quiet the crowd with their kindness as those gathered say, "Ah, yes, the Quakers have arrived." We have seen firsthand the power of what happens when people who are grounded in reason and compassion, though they identify with no religious tradition, constructively inspire us to consider a sophisticated ethical position. We say, "Oh, good, the Scientists"—or the Ethicists, or the Professors, or whoever they are—"have arrived."

There is an essential leadership attribute that each of these groups of people embody. They choose who they are *being* while deciding what they are doing. Most of justice work is centered around doing—strategizing, protesting, mobilizing. Effective leaders also know how to *lead by being*; they lead by being kind and empathetic and understanding and creative. They no longer spend all their energy on doing and doing and doing justice; they spend an equal amount on training themselves how to use their very presence to transform rather than escalate conflicts.

Many of us know intellectually that we must do more than just advocate for justice. We also emotionally intuit that there is something deeper and we long for a new way of being. However, we have yet to make the collective effort to first know what the *something* is and learn how to practice it on a daily basis. I believe the something is the moral imagination. It is compassion in action. It is leading by being kind and empathetic. It is a vision for using conflicts as opportunities for intimacy and mutual understanding.

I know that liberals aspire to be known as a people who are truly kind, but unfortunately we have allowed ourselves to be seen as irritable and inflexible—as liberal fundamentalists.

My position is not absolutist. There must be room for anger. Expressed constructively, anger can motivate, enliven, and empower. Heated, lively debates can serve as windows into our collective thinking and behavior. But we must never forget that anger is first and foremost a signal, not a solution. It can recalibrate our moral compass, helping us see that something dangerous lies ahead.

When anger becomes a solution, even our only solution, then our compass is pulled away from true north and we become lost and confused. To find our way home we must tend to our anger. Thích Nhất Hạnh teaches that when our house is on fire we must first extinguish the flames, not chase after those we perceive to be the arsonists.

We know this intellectually, and some religious leaders have learned to embody kindness in everything they do. Unfortunately, they are rare, and they often become disenchanted and begin to withdraw from the culture of aggression that can plague religious communities. Meanwhile, many of us continue to use our platforms, especially social media, to escalate conflicts, to smear those with whom we disagree, and to lurk in the shadow side of the imagination, ready to pounce on anyone who questions our self-proclaimed authority. We—I—spend much of our energy imagining how to win an argument, practicing how best to annihilate another's position, and rehearsing a speech with which to accept the award for "best performance in a leading role" in the dramas of our minds—dramas we can enact in congregational life.

In many religious communities in this country we routinely hear, "Where's my coffee? And why are those curtains crooked, and can you believe he wore that, and do you know what she said, that she said that she did what he said he would do but didn't do? And where's my Splenda?"

Preoccupations with idle chatter are a kind of self-poisoning. I think we should excommunicate such petty gossip. I think we should teach ourselves how to get out of the committee and into the streets.

But we cannot hit the streets intending to dominate and annihilate those we oppose in the same way that colonists assailed indigenous peoples. The goal is not to colonize the minds of those with whom we disagree, or to combat, with our ideas and ideologies, those we perceive as inferior. Instead, we can invite a variety of neighbors into a lively, civil dialogue. Through constructive exchanges and meaningful discussions, we are all changed. This goal assumes that the collective is wiser than the individual or sub-group. Truth is not a territory that we stake out. Truth-telling is a relational process of being intellectually honest with one another and being open to one another's insights. Individuals and groups can make truth by experimenting with the moral imagination.

People will find strength in these experiments if, week after week, gaggles of co-religionists invite one another into a new kind of game. It is a game that says that my win is not your loss; your failure is not my soapbox; your mistake is not my invitation to be your teacher, your judge, or your fire-and-brimstone preacher. It is not a game that hardens me to all that is wrong. It is a game that softens my senses. That is what religion requires of us, to soften to one another, time and time again.

Returning to the question posed by the organizers of the lecture series Vikram and I attended—would the world be better off without religion? Absolutely not, if religion is used to heal and not harm. When religious communities are deeply rooted in a culture of the moral imagination, then the world is better off. We can be people of such a religion, making religion truly liberating, behaving in ways that build one another up rather than tear down. We can do this by grounding our religious identity in everyday practices that invite us into a new way of being.

Each time we gather, someone among us will have the courage to cast a vision. And we will collectively ask whether such a vision is idealistic or realistic. And a few days later that same person will offer a confession and say, "I totally blew it." We will respond by saying, "That's what Tuesdays are for—to test our ideals." That is when we reach out a hand, offer a seat, and suggest pressing delete. In that moment the new game begins. We try again. Sometimes we win, and many times we fail. With each round we are given the chance to return home. We return to our religious home to meet people who inspire us to restore our moral imagination, and who remind us to also take out the trash.

In such exchanges with our personal spiritual trainers, we make it our highest priority to treat one another with the utmost respect. We know the purpose of our religion: The gathered community serves as a training ground—a moral training ground to save us from becoming what we set out against.

When we recount our Tuesday stories, and finally admit our part in fueling the flames, we begin to see a larger pattern. The pattern raises great questions: "Nate, if you treat a stranger that way, how are you treating your partner? How are you treating your family? Nate, how are you treating yourself?"

When we hold one another in care, in one another's presence, we create a space to be honest, to be vulnerable. That is what it means to be called to do justice work. Justice work does not consist of acts that harden us to one another's suffering; it is a way of being that requires that we soften to one another with each breath.

When we blow it on a Tuesday, we may find refuge on a Sunday in liberating religious traditions that both nurture us and challenge us to be our best selves. We may find refuge in putting down the torches and choosing not to storm the castle. We may even have the courage to stop chasing the people we think of as arsonists and choose not to fuel the fire, even one we consciously or subconsciously helped to create.

MY GOD!

My full name is Nathan Coffey Collier Wolf Emerson Walker. My friends call me Nate. Kids call me Nato-potato. Many call me lucky to have been born on New Year's Eve.

My mom, Mary Coffey Jr., never spoke of seeing fireworks or singing "Auld Lang Syne" or kissing her way into the New Year when I was born. She told me that she had felt profoundly alone in Munich, Germany, and so she named me Nathan, because of its meaning, *gift*. Two years earlier, my mom had traveled to Europe for several reasons, including being inspired by *The Sound of Music*. She left her home in Carson City, Nevada, with a suitcase in one hand and a guitar case in the other, determined to dance in the Alps. Her high school sweetheart, Mike Collier, later met her in Europe. I was conceived; they separated; I was born. I think Julie Andrews made me gay.

I was a year old when my mom returned home, and while enrolled in a Nevada history class in Reno, she met her true love, Steve Walker. He formally adopted me when they married, a few months before my fourth birthday; then came my remarkable brother, Kenny.

Our folks did not raise us in a religious home, but they were devotional. Most weekends, they went horseback riding in the Sierra Nevadas. I never explicitly asked them, but always suspected they were the founders of the Equestrian religion. Some of my fondest memories are of camping with my family. We would sit around the fire and tell stories; my mom and brother would play their guitars, and we would sing songs. My dad, like a good cowboy, would recite poetry, then we would sit in silence and make wishes upon falling stars. Surrounded by the beauty of Lake Tahoe, we found that the material, the tangible, the natural catalyzed our reflections on the nonmaterial aspects of life.

But there came a time when nature could not address social questions. When I was fifteen, my dad found a love letter in my pants pocket written to my boyfriend. It was 1992 and I had been partially out the closet for a year. It was northern Nevada.

My grandmother, Mary Coffey Sr., offered a very religious response to my coming out. She grabbed my hand and said, "I hear there's a lesbian up at the Unitarian fellowship." And off we went to meet the lesbian!

This visit had a profound effect on my decision, in my late twenties, to enroll in seminary and become a Unitarian Universalist minister. Before graduate school, I had gone to Emerson College in Boston. When I was making my decision to move to Boston, my mom and I talked about how my original middle name had been Emerson. When Dad adopted me, my name was legally changed from Nathan Emerson Coffey to Nathan Coffey Walker so that I could carry both my parents' names.

I chose Emerson College for two reasons. First, it offered a duel BFA program in Theatre Education and Musical Theatre Performance—thank you, Julie Andrews! Second, it had a study-abroad program in southern Holland, allowing me to travel to Germany and find my biological father.

From as early as I can remember, I had always known about Mike Collier. When I was in fifth or sixth grade, my parents told me that he had come to visit. They asked me if I wanted to meet him and I declined. It was not until I was twenty years old that I finally had the courage to meet him for the first time.

❖ ❖ ❖

Walking off the train platform in Heidelberg, Germany, I scanned the station to find the man, who, of course, would have to look exactly like Robert Redford. I just knew he would have perfect hair, his voice would sound like a disk jockey's, and he would smell like Old Spice.

As I clutched my backpack straps, my breath faltered. I wondered what he would think of me. I was not looking for another dad—Steve was the best father any child could have—but I questioned whether Mike would deem me worthy to be his son. I was nervous and could not help but remember my mom's letter to him, which he had received a few weeks earlier.

"Are you sitting down, Mike?" she wrote to prepare him. "There are three things you should know. First, Nathan is ready to meet you. Second, he's living about an hour away from you. Third, he's gay."

I appreciated her preparing him with that news, so that I would not have to face his potential shock. But at that moment on the train platform, my imagination ran amok: "What if he didn't show up? What if he didn't want to meet a faggot of a son?" I asked myself. I was terrified, and my negative self-talk took over.

Then, from across the waiting room, I heard my name being called. "Nathan?"

The whole experience is blurry to me now. I remember seeing a man wave. I remember hearing him laugh nervously. I laughed, too. He opened his long arms and said, "Wow, dude, this is totally cool."

I awkwardly replied, "Uh, yeah. Totally cool."

Did he smell like incense? Was he wearing tie-dye, or did he only seem to be trapped in the sixties? He was being kind, while I was being an ass. Why was I judging him?

Then he said, "This is, like, crazy. I've been waiting for this for, like, forever, man."

"Thanks, Mike," I said, to which he replied, "Call me Spike."

Spike? WTF? That confirmed it. I had officially time warped into the great psychedelic cosmos where a hippie in Woodstock,

New York, had conceived a child with a surfer from Santa Cruz, California, given birth to my biological father, and allowed him to roam Europe.

Let's just say he was not at all what I had expected. Nor, I assumed, was I what he had expected. "I'm sure he wasn't expecting to meet a fag," I remember saying to myself.

I see now that my unfair judgments of us both were windows into my insecurity and immaturity.

I barely remember walking toward his sports car, but I do remember that he drove fast, which was fun and to be expected in Germany. He cracked me up and set me at ease with nervous jokes as he pulled up to the military base where he taught golf. I wondered if *golf* was code for *international drug dealer*. Turns out, he really did teach golf. Go figure.

Mike lived in a military cabin with his girlfriend of eleven years. She embodied her name, Joy. "You have his smile," she said to me. Their home was cozy and decorated with exotic trinkets from their world travels. They set their slideshows to music, and their stories were full of adventure and humor. Like my parents, they had found true love, which ultimately set me at ease. I came to respect them as individuals and as a couple and felt grateful that my mom and Mike had not stayed together, for they would have been miserable and never met their true loves.

I was impressed by how Mike and Joy welcomed me. He even told a few gay jokes to show me that he was, as he said, "cool with all that." They both were unconditionally accepting. My fears were unfounded, and my judgmental first impressions said more about me than about him. He was clearly the life of the party and innately kind. "Good man," I said to myself as I went to sleep on their couch. "They've built a great life together—just like my parents." My knowing this had a transformative effect, as if my DNA had become aligned for the first time.

As the weekend progressed, the Monet of my life began to come into focus. I was finally meeting the person who until then had been performing in the basement of my mind, like a character in a silent film. He was not the man my subconscious imagination had created. My biological father was a bright, adventurous, hippy golf dude who went by the nickname "Spike."

He was sensitive and, like me, used a lot of negative self-talk. He worried that my mom had let me believe that Steve was my biological father. I showed him otherwise; I had always known about him and had always had the choice to meet him when I was ready. He was relieved by this news and seemed to respect my upbringing.

Mike told me that when he was twenty years old, he met his own biological father for the first time: Chuck Wolf was his name. Chuck was Cherokee and had worked as a stuntman in Hollywood. Mike's mother, Flo, remarried and took the name Collier, which is why Collier and Wolf are a part of my lineage. I have since become close with Flo. She is a lovely person—spiritual and generous.

Mike had stayed in Germany all those years. He had built a lovely life with Joy and was passionate about world affairs and animals. For some reason, these things surprised me. I was most perplexed to see him do dishes. How pedestrian. Then it hit me— "He's just a guy." He had insecurities and unmet aspirations. He was just a man. How could that be? That wasn't the being I had been praying to my entire life.

"Oh my God," I realized. "He is not my God."

That was the first moment I breached into reality—as if surfacing from a deep ocean, gasping for air for the first time. Breathing hurt but eventually gave me life. My initial breaths helped me realize that the movie star in the sky that I had been talking to my entire life was a figment of my imagination.

In much of that God-talk, I had been subconsciously trying to make proud the father figure I imagined. This is odd, considering that both my mom and dad were unconditionally supportive of my brother and me. I never felt like I was lacking anything, and yet my imagination lured me with a mirage of my own making.

The only way I know to translate this experience to others is through an analogy. I liken it to the way my theist friends describe their prayer life. The difference is that for them, God is not imag ined. God is a very real experience for them, because their devotional practices are conscious acts. They have a deep and personal relationship with their understanding of the divine. My prayers were just as rich and intimate, I suspect, but they were subconscious. I became conscious of them when I met a very real human being. My theist friends, on the other hand, already have a conscious relationship with their God and talk about that relationship openly. I only started to do the same after I realized that my construct was imagined.

You see, I never formally learned how to pray. Maybe it was because of my nonreligious (Equestrian) upbringing or because of my disdain for those who claimed to use spiritual disciplines to "cure" homosexuality, but I never learned a formal theology. I was, thankfully, given the autonomy to seek truth independently and responsibly, without the influence of any particular religion. But I did not have to explain my imagination to others, and so I did not become conscious of it. My unexamined imagination led me to construct a personal relationship with the God of my understanding—a subconscious vision of my biological father.

❖ ❖ ❖

Throughout my life, my mom has been my best friend. She is my first love, and we have a deep and lasting bond. She used to say, "Honey, you're a natural." I loved when she said that because I knew *The Natural*, staring Robert Redford, was one of her favorite movies.

I thought that because my biological father was an athlete, maybe he would be proud of me for playing baseball. I played left field and would often daydream, saying to him in my mind, "Thanks for making me a natural. Watch me. I can do a front flip, and I can even stand on my hands for a whole minute." My coach would yell, "Pay attention, Nathan!" That seemed to be his mantra, especially when on another day I walked by the dugout during a practice session and a wild pitch went straight toward my face and broke my jaw.

I was in sixth grade at the time. I remember screaming not only because of the pain of my shattered bone but also because I had let him down—not my coach, my biological father. How could I be a natural with a broken jaw? I could never be his "Wonderboy" now. What if he were in the stands that day, watching, in some *Field of Dreams* kind of way? What if he showed up a few weeks later and I could not talk with him because I had wires locking my jaw shut? After that, I never played baseball again.

I later convinced my folks to enroll me in Taekwondo. My mom had told me years earlier that my biological father was a superior athlete and that he had a black belt in karate. While practicing the kicks and blocks, I told him over and over in my mind, "I'm gonna make you proud. Look at me now." I even asked, "Would you be happy if they give me a yellow belt?" When the teacher gave me a compliment, my thoughts went to him: "Don't praise me, praise Mike. I have the genes of Mike Collier," I would say to myself.

I stopped doing that when I overheard a kid say to our instructor, "Don't praise me, praise Jesus." He later told me that he was praying for the strength to "kick the shit out of Sam," one of our teammates.

As the sparring increased, so did the unexpected tears. I knew that once we stopped using the pads, the kicks would hurt badly. I watched the Jesus kid's face contort as he fought me. I was terrified by his religious rage. I did not want to fight him—or his Jesus. Sure, you can count on me to push my younger brother around, but that was just for fun. I did not want to be hurt again and did not want to hurt anyone else. And so I just stopped going. I felt ashamed and internally pleaded to my imagined father for forgiveness: "Please don't be disappointed."

❖   ❖   ❖

Before I got to know my biological father, my imagination was preoccupied with subconsciously trying to please this God-like figure. Meeting Mike Spike destroyed this construct, and that trauma ultimately became a moment of liberation. I finally became aware of my ability to create an image of God that mirrored my expectations of my biological father. Very Freudian, isn't it?

After I met him, a deafening silence settled into the corners of my mind. My vague and ethereal understanding of Mike Collier was replaced with a concrete image of a man standing in the Heidelberg train station. From that moment, my instinct to pray disappeared completely. I did not know whom to address. I did not know how to start my plea. I was not about to petition Mike for his acceptance, or appeal to his forgiving heart, or express my adoration or remorse, or give thanks. Certainly it was not an option to cry out, "Lord Redford, grant me the serenity to accept the things that cannot be changed, the courage to change the things that make me insane, and the wisdom to know the difference. In the name of Fraulein Maria, amen."

Meeting Mike Collier twenty years ago was like what some pastoral counselors call a death-of-God experience. That may be why prayer has proved to be a struggle for me ever since.

Even after I entered seminary, even after I became a minister, my religious life was devoid of personal prayer. Why pray? To whom? If I became a theist, would I return to talking to the imaginary construct in my mind? Is it poor form on my part to conflate my feelings with the experiences of those who have a personal relationship with a deity? Is it poor form on their part to expect me to pray to theirs? Why participate in a spiritual discipline that goes against my direct experience?

And yet the practice of ministry led me to encounter people who were suffering greatly. Their suffering became an invitation to enter into their rich internal lives. In those moments, not praying was not an option.

While I was serving families in a pediatric intensive care unit as a chaplain one summer, ten children in the unit died. In those moments, I discovered that I was a natural. My prayers were passionate, poetic, and sincere. I prayed for and with the parents. I prayed for and with the surviving siblings. I prayed not because

I believed in the supernatural, but because I believed in their experience of their God, and I believed in my ability to practice the moral imagination.

In those moments, I found peace in learning to articulate what the patients and their families believed by using their own theological rhetoric. I learned the language they used to express their beliefs and found ways to help them speak authentically in it. I simply believed that their faith, not the absence of mine, would make them well. I opened my mind to hear them speak of their direct experiences. "Direct experience of transcending mystery and wonder" is one of the six Sources of Unitarian Universalism. I intended to simply bask in the wonder and beauty of their personal theology—without judgment, without coercion. I trained myself to use my imagination to enter into their religious worldviews and to see their belief systems as authentic expressions of their selves. My role became clear: not to convince them of my beliefs or my disbeliefs but to help them responsibly express their own. If they were using their thoughts to help and not harm, they had my full and unconditional attention.

I was in no position to tell them that their faith was anything but true, unless, of course, they used their beliefs to hurt themselves or others. That was my bottom line. I believed they were capable of engaging in a free and responsible search for truth and meaning—and this search is one of the seven Principles affirmed by Unitarian Universalist congregations. I did not need to agree with these families to understand them. I did not need to adopt their God-talk for myself. I simply needed to learn to speak it, to better help them give voice to their suffering.

It was as if I needed to learn to speak German in order to help someone living in Germany to learn about German culture. Doing this would not require me to renounce my U.S. citizenship. I saw myself as an ambassador, a translator, first learning their theological language and then helping them express their beliefs on their own terms.

These encounters have become some of my most profound triumphs in my lifelong experiments with the moral imagination

My ability to imagine myself as a theist did not make me one; rather, it helped me be a better humanist, aware that the religious impulse is a human one.

❖　❖　❖

I wonder what it would have been like if someone had approached me years before my encounter with my biological father in Heidelberg and told me that my prayers were false projections of a romanticized understanding of him. I would not have—indeed, could not have—comprehended such an idea. Only after I experienced the absence of that construct did it become clear to me that it had been born from the shadow side of my imagination. I romanticized Mike Collier out of his humanity and, in doing so, made him out to be "the other." Romanticizing him was a profound failure in my pursuit of the moral imagination.

I make this confession to set the stage for a larger conversation about the complex ways that people use the imagination, consciously or subconsciously. For me, prayer began as a creative internal dialogue, but this dialogue evaporated when I met Spike. My struggle with prayer became one of the reasons I enrolled in seminary—to work out one of my most private moral dilemmas. Seminary, and ultimately ministry, allowed me to formally claim myself as a religious humanist and intentionally learn from people from a diverse array of religious traditions.

My faith journey has led me to see how the shadow side of the imagination is cultivated when we are preoccupied with thoughts that can cause harm to either others or ourselves. For example, I experienced pain when the illusion of "my God" came face to face with the humanity of Mike Collier. However, when used intentionally, the imagination can also heal, as shown in my attempt to imagine myself in the shoes of those families that were suffering in the intensive care unit.

Who would have thought that this kid, born to a single mother, would make a pilgrimage into his ancestry as a young adult only to discover the power and complexity of his imagination? I have learned that to evoke the moral imagination is to see the world through another's eyes, which you have already begun to do by reading my birth story. You have already started to use your curiosity to imagine, to empathize with, and to understand the man behind the name Nathan Coffey Collier Wolf Emerson Walker— the gay kid who was born in the Alps, raised in the Sierras, and once had a death-of-God experience that inspired him to become a humanist Unitarian Universalist minister and to write about the moral imagination as an everyday spiritual practice.

I must admit: My birth story is nothing compared with the following death story.

REIMAGINING RWANDA

How would you respond if I told you that my colleague's family was murdered by his neighbors? Given this stark information, what picture does your imagination give you of his neighbors? How does it change when you learn that his family members were not the only victims—that tens of thousands of other people were similarly killed by their neighbors that month? When you learn that there were priests, rabbis, and sheiks in those neighborhoods who allowed their houses of worship to be places of slaughter? What do you feel? What does your gut say about these religious leaders? What do you think of the public officials, teachers, and doctors who also participated in this genocide?

I beckon you to kindle your imagination as a spiritual practice as we explore the genocide of the Tutsi people in the African country of Rwanda. In the spring of 1994, the United Nations and the Clinton administration were acutely aware that leaders of the Hutu-dominated Rwandan government were strategizing a nationwide execution of the Tutsi people. The Hutus used the radio to broadcast propaganda that made clear the Tutsis were to be feared. They were to be eliminated. Even if they were neighbors or spouses, teachers or strangers, the Tutsis were to be killed. The Hutu leaders were convinced that the Tutsis were out to destroy them. The only possible way to "defend" their land was to purge the earth of their existence.

They almost succeeded. According to the United Nations, approximately eight hundred thousand Tutsis were massacred in a hundred-day period. Imagine.

❖ ❖ ❖

I came to learn many details about this genocide while serving as a coordinator for the Remembering Rwanda conference sponsored by the Institute for the Study of Genocide, which was held at Union Theological Seminary in New York City in 2004. There, my Rwandan colleague spoke of his experience.

He was studying in the U.S. when the genocide began, and he returned to his home to speak with his sister. There he learned that she had used her position as a public official to order the death of their other sister because she had married a Tutsi. Family members were killing each other; some even murdered their mixed-ethnicity offspring. Distraught, my colleague struggled to imagine how his homeland was strewn with dead bodies—in the streets, in the churches, at the borders. Everywhere.

His conference address was haunting. He had been engaging in a psychiatric study of Hutu people who admitted to having murdered Tutsis. We read aloud the surveys he had administered, surveys that asked the most horrific questions. But the questions were nothing compared to the answers:

Did you kill a Tutsi?
Yes.
How many?
Dozens.
Did you kill a child?
Yes.
How many?
Four.
Did you rape a Tutsi?
Yes.
Did you witness someone else rape a Tutsi?

Yes.
Did you personally know the people you killed and raped?
Yes.
Who were they?
My coworkers. My neighbors.

My colleague showed us one survey, which he said had been completed by a man while they sat across a table from one another.
How many people did you kill?
Eight.
Do you know the names of the people you killed?
Yes.
His sister's name was third on the list.

❖ ❖ ❖

Imagine sitting across a table from the person who murdered your sister.

The perpetrator kept explaining that the person who killed her was also dead now. He was a new person, he said. He was not that person. He was not that man, he pleaded. He was a new man.

This man had previously used the shadow side of his imagination to connect himself to the community's goal of eradicating the Tutsis. But once the community became aware of what it had become, he began to use his imagination to reinvent himself, imagining himself as a meaningful participant in his community and no longer a threat to society.

His imagination once plummeted him into the bowels of a genocide, where he became a murderer. Reflecting upon his actions, and those of his country, led him to acknowledge the shadow side of his imagination and to begin to use his moral imagination to save himself and his country.

❖ ❖ ❖

In the last chapter, I shared the story of my birth. In this one I tell the story of these deaths. I do so for a single purpose, to ask a simple question: How do, and how will, others use their imagination?

Will people follow in my footsteps and romanticize another as their God? Will they use their imagination to make a person out to be entirely inhuman? Or will they follow in the footsteps of the Dutch colonists who used their imaginations to construct two races—the Hutu and Tutsi peoples? The Tutsis were those whom they deemed lighter-skinned, worthy of education, and fit to rule Rwanda. Eventually, through the democratization of the country, the Hutu majority overthrew the Tutsis, and once in power, the Hutus used their imaginations to exterminate their neighbors, even members of their own family.

The Hutus' collective imagination was dominated by fear. They feared the Tutsis and therefore stripped them of their inherent worth and justified their annihilation. Using an immoral imagination, they not only robbed others of life, they also stripped themselves of dignity. Yet, after it was over, those who were involved in these horrific acts began to imagine a new life for themselves. They first admitted their participation in the genocide and tried to reconcile their relationships with the surviving family members while simultaneously reimagining themselves as a united Rwanda, promising never again to use their imagination to harm.

When we fail to see one another's humanity, we cannot use our imagination responsibly. We are incapable of using our moral imagination when we are not able to understand what it must be like to see the world through another person's eyes. Failing in this, we fail to cultivate empathy and compassion, and our imagination becomes imprisoned by discriminatory thoughts.

The story of Rwanda is an all-too-common story of the human ability to invidiously discriminate. Yet humanity, like all of nature, is diverse. If diversity is our true nature, why do we continue to feed the discriminatory mind and fear difference? Why do we fear "the other"?

Recall Robert Schreiter's seven ways of otherizing: we may demonize, romanticize, colonize, generalize, trivialize, homogenize, or vaporize the other. I romanticized my father; the Hutus demonized the Tutsis (and moderate Hutus, as well). In both cases, fear led to otherizing and to violence—emotional in one instance, horrifically literal in the other.

Otherness is a root of violence. We can and must reflect upon this truth: Violent cycles begin when fear and bigotry plague the imagination; but, with insight, the mind can use the moral imagination as an ethical discipline to transform any conflict. When used mindfully, this everyday practice can evoke empathy and compassion in oneself and in another.

At key points in history, leaders have inspired us to imagine new ways of being together. Some such leaders were born from the apartheid state of South Africa.

WITH YOU ALWAYS

will always remember his presence, the world leader calling for equality. I will also always remember the presence of the stranger who died in front of me on an airplane. These two stories, one of rebirth and one of death, continue to stimulate my moral imagination.

The first story is of a man who risked his life to actualize his vision of a country free from racial segregation, a man committed to awakening the moral imagination of a country caged by apartheid: the ever-prophetic former president of South Africa, Nelson Mandela.

The second is about two women who tried to learn about the last moments of their father's life—their father who died on American Airlines flight 19 from New York to Los Angeles.

These true stories are not isolated events in my life; they are intimately woven into my moral fabric. The death occurred one month after I had enrolled in seminary; Mandela spoke in New York a week before my graduation. Each solidified my ministerial formation and illuminated my understanding of the moral imagination.

❖ ❖ ❖

A few hours before I submitted the last exam of my last year of seminary, the church bells rang and organ pipes made the pen quake on my desk. You see, my dorm room shared a wall with the organ of Riverside Church in New York: a famous nineteen-story cathedral, across from Grant's Tomb, which served the Harlem community. Its private entrance, often used by clergy and guest speakers, was directly under my window. I glanced out the window, but hardly blinked when I saw Secret Service agents next to a sleek black limousine. After all, famous people were constantly coming to visit this historic church. Then my cell phone rang. My friend Baranda was panting on the line: "Nelson Mandela is speaking at Riverside!"

"When?" I asked, and she gasped, in a voice filled with smothered excitement, "Right now. Get over here!"

I stared at my half-baked take-home exam—the last one of my seminary career—which was due in forty minutes. This, I supposed, was what one would call a moral dilemma. I could either see Nelson Mandela or graduate from seminary. It must have been the ominous sounds of the organ that helped me realize that this hooky-playing reverend-to-be was one wall away from greatness. I threw on my tennies and ball cap and ran out.

❖   ❖   ❖

The descendants of southern Africa's Dutch colonists, the Afrikaners, coined the term *apartheid*, meaning "apartness." In 1948, the country of South Africa was officially separated into four racial categories: White, Indian, Coloured, and African/Black. Put simply, the lighter your skin, the more civil rights you received. This was the same year that the "great soul," Mohandas Gandhi, was assassinated; years earlier, he had nonviolently led Indians in South Africa to protest against the early stages of apartheid.

Another historic leader emerged from this invidious discrimination. Nelson Mandela was born in 1918, the year World War I ended and an influenza epidemic killed millions worldwide. His father died of an undiagnosed lung disease when Nelson was nine years old, and in 2002, Nelson's own son became a victim of our present-day epidemic: AIDS. In 1952 Mandela courageously organized the Defiance Campaign against Unjust Laws for the African National Congress and other organizations, to protest the system of apartheid. This and similar work led him to be charged twice with treason. After twelve years of resistance, Mandela was sentenced to life in prison.

❖   ❖   ❖

I entered the neo-Gothic church that day to hear James Forbes begin the service by reflecting upon the day when Mandela first came to Riverside Church. In 1990, soon after being released from prison after twenty-seven years, Mandela came to Harlem, the heart of black America, to proclaim South Africa free from apartheid. Forbes explained that Mandela had returned to Riverside to say his final goodbyes, because this would probably be his last visit to the States.

Harry Belafonte proudly introduced his friend Mandela after a roaring celebration, with music by the South African Harlem Choir and the Harlem Boys Choir, followed by an eloquent speech from Congressman Charles Rangel. Dressed in a vibrant yellow shirt that contrasted with his crisp white hair, Mandela wore a smile that stretched from sea to sea. Humbly, he delivered a short, unassuming speech, saying simply, "I will not be traveling again to the United States. I am turning eighty-seven in July, and people our age should not be traveling across oceans." He came to say goodbye. He came to Harlem to say simply, "I am with you always."

My eyes watered. The same phrase can be found in the last sentence of the Gospel of Matthew. I *did* learn something from my class—my class! I sneaked out of the sanctuary, ran back to get my things, and barreled through the bowels of the seminary, only to burst out laughing at the sign on the classroom door: "The in-class portion of the final exam is postponed. Go see Mandela!"

The memory of that sign will also stay with me always.

❖   ❖   ❖

I had finished my fifth week of seminary and was flying from New York to Los Angeles when the man sitting in front of me died.

No one realized this until after we landed and the woman sitting next to him tried to leave her window seat. I could see from behind that he was not moving. I placed my hand on his shoulders to rouse him. I checked for a pulse on his neck and then over his heart. I lifted his arm to check his wrist. It had turned purple. Another man helped the woman over the body as yet another man helped me lay his body in the aisle. I started doing CPR and then the flight attendants relieved me, the paramedics relieved them, and soon enough they pronounced him dead.

By this time, there were only a few of us left on the plane, including the flight attendants and paramedics. I turned to a stewardess and asked, "Should we bless the body?" She started crying. "We need a minister for that." I was wearing a ball cap and jeans. I pulled out my student identification card and said, tentatively, "I'm in seminary."

She sighed with relief. I stiffened under the pressure I had brought upon myself, and began to scoot closer again, past the rows of seats. The stewardess said, "This minister will bless the body."

While everyone gathered, my eyes fell upon the man lying in the middle of the aisle. What kind of prayer, if any, was appropriate for me to offer for this stranger? He is no stranger, my conscience reminded me. He seemed to be Eastern Indian, or maybe Native American. What did any of us standing around him know of his culture, his religion, his beliefs? I wanted my imagination to help me know him, but how was that possible? Was it presumptuous of me to bless his body? What if he was not religious or spiritual at all? But those around me seemed to be expressing their faith.

One stewardess crossed herself; one of the bystanders was wearing a yarmulke; one of the paramedics was impatient, tapping his knuckles on the tray table. So I tried to discern how to honor the man who died, even though I was unaware of his own beliefs and sensitive to the religious diversity of the witnesses. I began by saying, "God of many names and one abundant love . . . may this soul. . . ."

I do not remember everything that fell from my lips, but I recall hesitating before closing the prayer. "In the name . . . in the name . . ." In the name of *what*? American Airlines? "In the name . . . of all that is holy. Amen."

One woman burst into tears. The paramedic rolled his eyes. Another woman put her hand on my shoulder and said, "Thank you."

I stayed with the flight attendants for about an hour and counseled them as they completed their reports. One woman in particular had recently lost her father and could not stop crying. Filling out the death certificate was impossible for her. I asked her colleague to help her as she talked about her father. I was kneeling at her feet, listening. While hearing her story, and listening to others console her and speak of their own loss, I was watching myself: so calm, so peaceful. This was a traumatic event, Nate, why aren't the tears rolling down your face? I was at peace. I felt a sense of purpose and clarity about the moment. And then I realized that my connecting flight had most likely taken off.

I said my goodbyes and briskly walked through the jetway toward the bustling airport. I then started to bawl. I did not know this man, but I mourned for him, not because he was my friend or because we had much in common but because he was human. I kept contrasting the discolored skin of his wrist with his peaceful appearance during my prayer. I did not feel that I had blessed him; I had simply acknowledged his presence, which was a blessing to us all.

I cried until I reached my connecting gate, only to see that the flight was delayed. I found that to be strange, considering the weather was perfect. The delay was due to "technical difficulties," said the stewardess as she welcomed me on the plane.

The door closed, the cabin was secure as we ascended into the western sky. I said hello to the women next to me. She impulsively replied, "I'm on my way to my brother's funeral." I was beyond shock at this point. I was fully alive. I never told her what had happened just moments before—she deserved my full attention. She talked and cried nearly all the way to the Reno/Tahoe airport, until being silenced by the sunset illuminating the Sierras.

❖ ❖ ❖

Two and a half years later, a month before my seminary graduation, the following email arrived in my inbox from a woman I did not know:

> To: Nate Walker
> Sent: Saturday, April 23, 2005 3:52 PM
> Subject: Regarding Reflection on a Personal Experience
>
> Dear Mr. Walker,
>
> I recently came across your memorial online for a Mr. Brijlall, who passed away on an American Airlines flight. Your essay did not note the date of this encounter, but my father passed away on October 9, 2002 on an American Airlines flight to Los Angeles. I would like to know if you were in fact on this flight, and if so my family would like to thank you sincerely for the efforts you made to save his life and for your kind words. If you would like to contact me, I can be reached at this email address.

The deceased man had indeed been her father. She had found my website by doing an Internet search for her last name. We exchanged a few emails and a phone call. She lived in Brooklyn, and a few weeks later she and her sister came to my seminary dorm room. They sat on my futon, and over tea we talked at length about their father. He seemed to have been a remarkable human being.

Although Mr. Brijlall was raised in India and was a practicing Hindu, he had decided to raise his children Christian, to better integrate them into American society. We talked at length about their family's belief system: they seemed to authentically honor their father's Hindu heritage while also finding comfort in the spiritual practices of Christianity.

We also talked about Mr. Brijlall's love of traveling, of culture, and of people. Throughout his life he crossed many borders, experienced many divides, and yet lived as if there were no separation between himself and others. He had traveled to over a hundred countries, and he had passed away while doing what he loved.

As we were clearing our cups, we heard the organ pipes from next door. I walked them outside, where we said our goodbyes, then I returned to my desk to complete my final seminary exam. As I did so, the Secret Service began to gather outside my window, and Nelson Mandela entered Riverside Church.

❖ ❖ ❖

I retell these stories to say simply that Mr. Brijlall's presence and the words of Mr. Mandela will be with me always.

Nelson Mandela was a man who captured the moral imagination of a country and inspired its people to adopt policies that reflected the belief that all of us are worthy of equal treatment under the law. His years of sacrifice and his ability to see no one as "other" freed a country from racial segregation. His use of the moral imagination emancipated a country from the bowels of an imagination that found ways to picture certain people as inferior, and therefore less worthy of civil rights.

This same system of injustice was the fertile soil in which grew an Indian man's imagination about ways to nonviolently resist the discriminatory mindset of those in power. Mohandas Gandhi spent his days experimenting with ways to couple truth and love. His legacy led generations of Indians to prosper and become world citizens, like Mr. Brijlall.

My encounter with this man on the airplane became an opportunity to care for another, aware that there is no stranger

He was a man whose body ceased to function; a man whose life was worth trying to save, regardless of his race or religion. We were at one with one another, and sharing this story online gave me the opportunity to be at one with his daughters. In this way, the healing power of the imagination atoned for all notions of separateness.

AT-ONE-MENT

The flames glowed their light from red and orange candles on the windowsill in my dorm in New York City. It was 2005, and I had kindled three red candles to represent the three million people who were dying each year from AIDS. The three orange candles symbolized the three million people who suffered each year from the diseases and deformities caused by the chemical warfare agent known as Agent Orange, used by the United States during the war in Vietnam. These seemingly unrelated calamities formed the basis for a meditative exercise of the imagination.

❖ ❖ ❖

It was Yom Kippur, the Day of Atonement, the day when Jews reflect upon their broken relationships and seek to right the wrongs they have committed against one another. I was heading to Kitchenette, a restaurant near 125th Street, to have brunch with two friends. One was studying at the Jewish Theological Seminary; the other had recently graduated from Union Theological Seminary and was preparing for her ordination as a Presbyterian minister. Over our meal, my curiosity was kindled by the distinction my colleagues were making between the Jewish and Christian uses of atonement.

The future rabbi explained that although the term *atonement* had only recently been added to versions of the Christian New Testament, the Hebrew scriptures historically used it to refer to reconciling conflicts in all our relations. He described atonement as a ritual that invites broken relationships to return to wholeness. The future pastor explained in turn that in traditional Christian theology, atonement occurs in that fateful moment when Jesus Christ is sacrificed on the cross, thus atoning for the sins of humanity.

I asked them about their shared Biblical stories in which God chose one set of people and cursed another with diseases, by which they were to atone for their sins. I had been doing research on children's Bibles, and shared with them a passage from a children's Haggadah in Sheryl Prenzlau's *Exodus: The Jewish Children's Bible* that contains a list of "15 good things God has done for us." The list includes these lines:

> *God punished the Egyptians.*
> *God killed the firstborn Egyptians.*
> *God gave us the Egyptians' gold and silver.*
> *God drowned the Egyptian soldiers in the Red Sea.*

I said, "It's worrisome to see that this violent language, not to mention the accompanying illustrations, teaches children to imagine a God who initiates violence against another and permits God's chosen people to steal."

At first my colleagues were defensive, using apologetic language to define the historical context of scripture, then to define scripture as metaphor. Finally, after much listening, I asked them, "Would you read this particular children's Bible to your children?" They both replied with a clear and sincere "No."

"Why?"

They both described the words and drawings as "scary." It scared me to think of how ideas of a vindictive and violent God could colonize the minds of children.

❖   ❖   ❖

My imagination was stimulated by this conversation, leading me to return to my dorm to apply these theologies of atonement to two contemporary catastrophes. I unpinned a red ribbon from a sports jacket that hung from my futon. I had worn it the night before during a public demonstration that sought to draw attention to the HIV/AIDS pandemic. In the jacket pocket hid my journal. I opened it up and wrote questions about atonement:

How do we become what we set out against? Does the belief in atonement seek to relieve suffering only to create more? Does the belief in a God that wills disease—uses disease to atone for human sin—perpetuate more suffering? Does a belief in a theology that portrays God as having a will and human attributes, such as rage and disappointment, lead believers to imagine themselves having the same attributes?

Do we still live in a society that says, "God told me you were to be feared and eliminated"? Or maybe it is subtler nowadays: "Our scripture says your behavior is bad. Therefore you brought the suffering upon yourself and are to blame for the suffering others now experience."

I wrote down some words written by Pope Benedict XVI before his election to the papacy, when he was Joseph Cardinal Ratzinger. He said in his 1992 letter to the U.S. Bishops that homosexuality is a "strong tendency ordered toward an intrinsic moral evil; and thus the inclination itself must be seen as an objective disorder." He went on to say that "the practice of homosexuality may seriously threaten the lives and well-being of a large number of people."

I then recalled the words of the Reverend Dr. Jerry Falwell, who agreed. "AIDS," Falwell preached, "is a lethal judgment of God on the sin of homosexuality and it is also the judgment of God on America for endorsing this vulgar, perverted, and reprobate lifestyle. . . . God also says those engaged in such homosexual acts will receive . . . 'due penalty of their error.' . . . [He is] bringing judgment against this wicked practice through AIDS."

I imagined my friends telling me, "Nate, these conservative theologies of atonement confuse the act of making amends with

God's act of punishing the sinner, and not all Christians and Jews do so." And I began to construct a dialogue in my mind, replying, "Yes. However, the response of these religious leaders is based on a shared theology that has imagined a God of Wrath who uses disease to punish; a God who uses disease to teach gay people about their sins; a God who uses suffering to punish humans for their transgressions; a God who wills some people and not others to suffer, so sinners can learn their lesson and atone for their sins. This belief system is a continuation of the same kinds of irresponsible and dangerous thoughts expressed in Prenzlau's children's Bible."

I wrote more questions in my journal:

Is atonement an effective theology to care for the loved ones of the 3 million people who died last year from AIDS? Is this the theology that will truly redeem those who are currently suffering in this pandemic?

I recorded related statistics, which led me to pose more questions.

Kofi Annan, then secretary-general of the United Nations, reported that about three-quarters of the world's AIDS deaths every year occur in Africa, most of them women. In the U.S., according to a 2005 report by the Centers for Disease Control and Prevention, women accounted for more than a quarter of all new HIV/AIDS diagnoses, with women of color most at risk. That year, HIV infection was the leading cause of death for black women ages 25–34. Are we going to tell these women that their disease is God's will? What do we say to the 5 million people who were infected with HIV in 2005? How do we make sense of the fact that African-American and Hispanic women together represented about 25 percent of all U.S. women in 2004, yet they accounted for an estimated 81 percent of AIDS diagnoses among women? Do we tell these women of color, if they are heterosexuals, that they are innocent victims; do we tell the gay and bisexual men that they are guilty? Do we tell these men that their sins will be atoned for through their suffering with AIDS? Do we tell the sinner that we love him but not his sin?

Or, I wondered, do we have the courage to ask whether a theology of atonement, which is based on belief in a God who wills suffering, can do more harm than good? Rather than reuniting those who suffer, does this belief system have the unintended consequence of dividing people into two groups—the chosen ones and the sinners? Or do we have the strength to say, "No—the belief that suffering is redemptive comes from the idea that God wills pain, and therefore permits the one who claims to know God's will to justify discrimination"?

❖ ❖ ❖

After a good night's sleep, I was less on edge at the next meal with my friends. I shared with them the questions that had occupied my mind. They were very respectful and practiced the spiritual disciplines of openness and loving speech, which gave me the space to present my own theological standpoint.

I said simply, "Do you think it is possible to imagine a redemptive theology: a theology of at-one-ment?"

As I said these words, my body opened and the scowl on my face lightened into a bright-eyed smile. I had finally struggled through the mental tangle that had led me to focus on my opposition rather than my vision. I chose now to use my mind to make meaning rather than demean another's beliefs. I began to create rather than deconstruct ideas, which left me feeling more relaxed.

I wrote the term *at-one-ment* on a paper napkin, a term I later learned was not uncommon. I then recited a remark of the Universalist and Unitarian minister and teacher Alfred S. Cole: "Give them, not hell, but hope and courage. Do not push them deeper into their theological despair, but preach the kindness and everlasting love of God."

I then turned to my Jewish friend and said, "You described the ritual of Yom Kippur to be the practice of beginning again in our relationships with one another. I'm wondering if we can begin anew with the theology of at-one-ment."

Rather than tell children stories of a wrathful God, can we articulate the wonder that comes with knowing that many people throughout history have experienced a transcending presence? Can we release ourselves from transferring our human emotions onto those things we do not yet understand, such as the complexity of diseases and human sexuality? Can we take responsibility for our own difficult emotions, such as anger and desire for revenge, and find authentic ways to transform our ability to hate and discriminate into ways to love and understand?

Drawing upon my own experience meeting my biological father, I asked further, "Is it possible that the transcending mystery, experienced by many cultures, moves beyond all human projections? If so, maybe there can be a theology that imagines the divine *without an ego*, an egoless deity that is not bound by human desire or the need to be obeyed."

I explained that this divine essence is not bound by human desire and want; this egoless, lower-case god does not have the capacity to choose you and not me. An egoless god uses suffering not as a solution but as a signal that another person is in pain. The goal, therefore, is to be at one with all those who are suffering. It is that simple: Another person's pain is enough for me to imagine myself as them and hopefully help relieve that suffering. A theology of at-one-ment views disease not as a punishment but as a biological malady, which calls us to prevent it from taking yet another life.

❖ ❖ ❖

Our meal went on for quite a while, as our meals together usually did. But this conversation was palpably different from our others. I honestly cannot remember their responses. I distinctly remember their faces, their body language, and even the sunlight that crawled from one side of the room to the other. I must have been so preoccupied with my own thoughts that theirs did not stick. I regret not having listened in the same way they listened to me pontificate about my questions.

I wondered, if we were to authentically and routinely apply this new theology in our daily lives, whether we might see that redemption comes when we commit ourselves to being at one with all who suffer. In the context of the AIDS pandemic, this means we are called to teach one another how to prevent the spread of sexually transmitted diseases; to teach our children that responsible intimacy is necessary to the preservation of life; to recognize the intersections of the oppression of gay people and of people of color; and to teach the world that everyone is worthy of love, health, and happiness—without exception.

Their attentive listening as I struggled with traditional theologies of atonement showed me how they practiced the moral imagination, showing their willingness to be at one with those who suffer.

❖ ❖ ❖

Months later I found myself resting my back against the chilled brick of the sanctuary of Community Church in midtown Manhattan, while listening to a series of speakers at a mid-week presentation. What I was hearing spurred me to think again about the predominant belief that God wills suffering. I wondered if this belief could be applied to diseases other than AIDS: Are they, too, intended to atone for human sin?

The speaker at that moment was talking about Hodgkin's disease, multiple myeloma, prostate cancer, soft-tissue sarcoma, spina bifida, and type 2 diabetes. "What do these and numerous birth defects and various cancers of the lung have in common?" she asked. "They can result from being exposed to Agent Orange, a code name for a colorless herbicide used by the U.S. military during the Vietnam War to defoliate the environment, to eliminate all sources of food, and to force the Vietnamese to surrender."

She quoted an article published in *Nature* titled "The Extent and Patterns of Usage of Agent Orange and Other Herbicides in Vietnam" that concluded that 3,181 Vietnamese hamlets were sprayed directly with Agent Orange, which contained TCDD, or dioxin, one of the most toxic chemicals known to science. That meant that "at least 2.1 million but perhaps as many as 4.8 million people would have been present during the spraying." The article went on to say that "another 1,430 hamlets were also sprayed, but we cannot estimate the population involved."

I remember how shallow my breath felt during these speeches. Presenter after presenter shared personal stories. The most memorable was from Ho Sy Hai, an army truck driver from Tai Binh who suffered from chronic hepatitis, ulcers, prostate cancer, and diabetes. He was sixty-one years old and explained that his wife had had several stillbirths, and of their four children born alive one had died of cancer at age five, two had become deaf and unable to speak, and one was mentally ill. Had the U.S. known the effect that dioxin would have on two generations?

One speaker quoted James Clary, a former senior scientist at the Chemical Weapons Branch of the U.S. Air Force: "When we initiated the herbicide program in the 1960s, we were aware of the potential for damage due to dioxin contamination in the herbicide. We were even aware that the military formulation had a higher dioxin concentration than the civilian version due to the lower cost and speed of manufacture. However, because the material was to be used on the 'enemy,' none of us were overly concerned."

I could not help but think of the shadow side of the imagination when reading about the belief that the enemy should be eliminated by any means possible.

Ho Sy Hai explained that the Vietnam Association for Victims of Agent Orange had filed a class action lawsuit against several U.S. companies that had developed and produced dioxin. In March, 2004, a judge had dismissed the suit because Agent Orange was not considered a poison under international law at the time it was being used. This is the same judge who presided over the 1984 case that resulted in the chemical companies that manufactured Agent Orange having to pay $180 million into a fund for U.S. veterans.

I came to understand that the Vietnamese were not the only victims of this chemical warfare. According to the Department of

Veterans Affairs, the government must presume that any veteran who served in Vietnam between January 9, 1962, and May 7, 1975, and has one of a specified set of diseases was exposed to herbicides and that the disease is thus connected to their service.

❖ ❖ ❖

On the subway ride home, the following questions made their way into my journal:

How would Pope Benedict and Reverend Falwell respond to diseases resulting from military service? Would they say they were humanity's doing or that God willed them to happen? If the responsibility lay with humanity, was God leading the U.S. military to act on the idea that Americans were the chosen ones and the Vietnamese were to be eliminated? Or, if God was accountable for this act, then was God punishing the veterans for their sins? Or maybe they are like the heterosexuals with AIDS—innocent victims. That would make the Vietnamese guilty because they were the "enemy," right? Who is guilty in the case of Agent Orange?

I believe we are. We are the American educators who irresponsibly used our imaginations to teach scientists to invent herbicidal chemical weapons; we are the American chemists who sold our innovations to the military; we are the American business leaders and shareholders who profited from the sale of dioxin; we are the elected politicians who justified an unjustifiable war; we are the U.S. military leaders who would do anything to exterminate the enemy.

We are the ones who collectively played God.

We once imagined a God of Wrath who inflicts diseases on the sinner; we once believed we were justified in doing God's work and exterminating our enemy at any cost. We once believed suffering could be redemptive. We became what we set out against.

I cannot help but wonder how it would be if religious leaders reversed this trend by making clear that any theology that is used to demean, to cause harm, or to provoke violence is simply illegitimate. Period.

In doing so, those seeking to restore dignity to our relationships would imagine a theology of at-one-ment. Theologians might find refuge in such a belief; they might proclaim an ever-present and transcendent egoless presence. Humanists might find themselves joining with theologians to articulate a philosophy of at-one-ment, calling us to use the moral imagination in our everyday interactions, policies, inventions; guiding us to heal the wounds of war. Together, religious and nonreligious people alike might find themselves simply being at one with all who suffer. In doing so, they would see that both the Vietnamese and the veterans have inherent worth and that no person is alien to our compassion.

I saw from firsthand experience how this practice of at-one-ment can be redemptive. At Community Church, two people made a simple exchange: A U.S. veteran and a Vietnamese civilian turned to one another, shook hands, and said, "How do you do?" In that exchange, two people, once at war, were now in solidarity around their common suffering. They came together to tell their stories; they came to speak the truth and to reconcile with one another.

I stood leaning against a pillar of the church and could not help but feel my body change. My shoulders, hunched for most of the lecture, had relaxed, while my shame for being an American remained potent. I was an observer, witnessing a simple exchange of compassion. I did not know either of them. I am not certain they knew one another before that moment. And yet they were at one with each other, just as they were with me.

❖ ❖ ❖

In their honor, I lit six candles that evening. I pinned an orange ribbon on the left breast of my sports jacket, and on the right a red ribbon. I put the jacket on, sat down, and wrote in my journal: *The space between these two ribbons holds my deepest aspiration—to be at one; to be at one is to ensure that no human being will ever suffer like Ho Sy Hai and his family; to be at one is to tell the AIDS victim,*

"No disease can diminish your inherent worth and dignity"; to be at one is to teach the world's scientists, inventors, and business leaders to never profit from killing; to be at one is to reform this nation from a unilateral global power into a country whose commitment to freedom is not simply a political slogan but a way of life; to be at one is to acknowledge that redemption comes when we imagine another's suffering as our own.

❖ ❖ ❖

I share these stories to remind us that theology, like the imagination, is a tool. It can be used to make meaning or to demean another. Therefore, we must constantly ask ourselves how we are using our imagination to articulate our beliefs. Are we basing it on the belief that some people are more worthy than others, and if so, what are the social consequences of such a belief? Is it responsible to articulate a theology that permits discrimination, or a public policy that permits the unbridled annihilation of people and the planet in the name of war, in the name of God?

When such beliefs creep into our minds, our words, our scriptures, then all that we hold dear becomes tainted by violence. Is that the message religions will pass on to children? Not if the leaders of those religions are trained to affirm the moral imagination as an everyday spiritual practice.

GET UP!

In the last month of my ministerial internship, one year after graduating from seminary, I received an email asking, "How can you possibly say that Romans 1:27 doesn't refer to homosexuality?" That was the entire email.

Romans 1:27 reads, in the New International Version, "In the same way the men also abandoned natural relations with women and were inflamed with lust for one another. Men committed shameful acts with other men."

I could not understand why I had gotten this message. And then I realized that it could be in response to one of my marriage-equality speeches posted on my website where I wrote that Romans does not refer to what we now know as homosexuality. There was a signature: Jay G. Smith, a senior executive for Operation Blessing International, a company founded by Pat Robertson, an evangelical minister who vehemently opposes gay rights. Why would one of Robertson's senior executives write to me, a ministerial intern?

I did some research. Smith's online biography explained that he had received his Master of Divinity degree from the Southern Baptist Theological Seminary thirteen years earlier, having previously spent six years as a Lieutenant in the U.S. Navy and two years as a Captain in the Air Force. He had been married for more than thirty years, had four children, and lived in Virginia. The mission of Operation Blessing was "to exemplify Christian compassion and benevolence while conforming to the highest standards of integrity to combat hunger and . . . physical affliction."

I shared this email with my colleagues and friends, wondering how others would respond. Or maybe they would not respond at all. They gave me a wide variety of suggestions, from "hit delete" to "tell him he's a bigot." I understood their bitterness but did not feel the same way.

I called my then partner. When I told him I was uncertain of how to reply to my questioner, he said, in his delightful British/Indian accent, "Sounds like his anger got the best of him." His wisdom and the depth of his compassion for this stranger moved me. Just before hanging up he recommended taking a walk: a great idea.

As I walked under a canopy of flowering trees in Riverside Park, a song kept playing in my mind. It was a Christian pop song by Donnie McClurkin that had been shared during an ecumenical worship service at seminary: *We fall down but we get up / For a saint is just a sinner / who falls down and gets up.*

I began to add my own lyrics to fit my own beliefs, and they became a chant for me, heard softly by those walking through the park: *We fall down but we get up. / For we're people with a vision / who fall down and get up.*

I returned home and composed the following reply:

Dear Reverend Smith,

Please accept my apology. I am sorry if my interpretation was offensive. I will respectfully respond to your email to, first, clarify my understanding of the Greek translation and, second, ask for your advice.

I meant to convey that my interpretation of Romans 1:27 refers to pagan orgies, promiscuity, infidelity, and deceit. I understand these words to hold a different meaning to fidelity between consenting adults.

Regardless of my interpretation, my intention is to understand your position. After reading your bio online, it is clear that your expertise as a minister and humanitarian has enhanced your biblical scholarship. In this context, my hope is to seek your advice about the continuation of the passage, line 1:32, that reads, "those who do such things deserve death" (NIV).

I ask this question in the context of my own story. Last Valentine's Day while on the New York City subway a feeling of peace came over me as my date offered me a gift. He gave me a single red rose. We were then approached by a man in a suit who spat on us.

I remember another time when we were walking down the street in Manhattan when a tour bus passed. We heard screaming and saw that the tourists were pointing in our direction. We looked behind us to see what was wrong and realized they were looking at us holding hands.

How can something as innocent as holding hands provoke so much aggression?

❖ ❖ ❖

I found myself getting emotional while composing this email and began to recall the story of my coming out.

I was fifteen years old and had taken my girlfriend, Rachel, outside our biology classroom, where we stood eating Hershey's Kisses on a wooden staircase. I said there was something that she needed to know. "Remember that problem of mine? The one we've been writing about? The one referred to as a green asterisk?"

Over the previous months we had written dozens of letters to one another, and the green asterisk had become a symbol for something that was nameless to me at the time.

I admitted, "I finally know what the asterisk means."

My eyes watered as I unwrapped a Hershey's Kiss; I used it as my chocolate ink, the railing as my paper. I wrote, "I am gay."

With a gasp, she cupped her hands to her face, paced, and wept

It was 1991, and we were in Northern Nevada. She was the daughter of an esteemed Christian minister, the man who gave me my first Bible. As tenth graders, we were involved in the youth group and would always sit in church together. After learning about my sexuality she approached her father. She shared the meaning of the green asterisk and they reread my letters together. His response was immediate: "Love him. Be his friend." He explained that the stress and fear of coming out could lead to thoughts of suicide and said, "Rachel, he might need you more than ever."

Little did either of them know of the suicide note, knife, and calendar hidden in my dresser.

❖　❖　❖

I returned to the church a few months later and found a pamphlet entitled "Healing Homosexuality through Prayer." What? I wondered if the ushers knew—had they put it there for me? I put it in Rachel's hands and asked, "What's this?" She did not know anything about it and was upset. I approached her father. He took it from my hand and crumpled it, shook his head with disgust, and put an affirming hand on my shoulder.

I have often wondered how my life would have turned out if their reactions had been different. Their unconditionally supportive response nurtured my self-worth and was the seed of my own ministerial formation. I found comfort in knowing their family always welcomed me into their home and their church.

My family was equally loving in their response a year later, as I have described before. After my dad found a love letter I had written to my boyfriend, my folks spent a few months talking with a therapist to figure out how best to approach me. My mom's cousin had been kicked out of the family when he came out, and he tried to take his life. That was their fear; little did they know how right they were to really think through their response. They did so with love and care. I will never forget them saying, "We just want you to know you always have a home." And, of course, my grandmother took me off to meet a lesbian. The knife in my dresser found its way back to the kitchen where it belonged.

❖ ❖ ❖

I continued my letter to the Reverend Smith, describing why I had left my home state.

I moved to New York City because in my home state, Nevada, I was denied the ability to adopt a child. The state-funded adoption agent clutched her cross and said, "You do not meet the definition of family."

My experience with discrimination was not bound by any one state, for I was at a blood bank in Manhattan the other day and discovered a federal law prohibits gay men from donating blood. How did it come to be that my life-giving blood could not be used to save another's life?

Instead, Reverend Smith, some people read the Bible as giving them permission to take my life. Is death deserved for engaging in a loving relationship that is celebrated with the passing of a rose?

I have to be honest, Reverend Smith. I am scared. I am frightened by the violence in our society. Last month, the chief of staff for New York State Senator Vincent Leibell told me to move out of the state if gay marriage was so important to me. Is that my fate, to be banished from one state to the next?

In these moments, one can find refuge in Biblical stories that dignify those who were exiled and persecuted. One can find refuge in Jewish and Christian teachings that show us how to love our neighbor. And, specific to this conversation, one can find refuge in the mission of your organization that makes the pledge "to break the cycle of suffering."

Do you have any advice on how to live this mission? As a religious leader, do you have any suggestions on how my life can be dedicated to addressing the hostility and violence that I experience in my everyday life?

Thank you for your time to write. I look forward to future dialogue.

Faithfully,
Nate

I pressed send while humming *We fall down but we get up. / For we're people with a vision / who fall down and get up.*

❖ ❖ ❖

Within two hours he replied.

"Nate: You ask some very good questions."

My jaw fell to the keyboard.

"I will do my best to formulate an answer," he continued. "However, I can't take time from work to do that. Let me also say I'm sorry for the ridicule and heckling you've been subjected to."

My eyes welled with tears. I thanked him for his quick reply.

Years have passed. I have not yet heard from him.

❖ ❖ ❖

There will be times when we receive hostile emails; people will heckle us from Manhattan tour buses; governments will say we are not worthy of adopting or donating blood, just like politicians sought to banish us to Massachusetts; and religious leaders will continue to recite biblical passages that condemn us to death.

What kind of response can we imagine? Maybe we can say,

- Get up! As a minister, Reverend Smith, you were called to break, not create, the cycle of suffering.
- Get up! As a government official, Senator Leibell, you took a vow to ensure that no American will ever be deprived of equal protection under the law.

- Get up! Children of Abraham, you are called to treat others as you wish to be treated.

Such an ethic applies to my own behavior. I have told my family and my religious community that when they see me stooping to hostility, when they witness me plummeting into bigotry, when they watch me use my power to exile, my hope is that they will have the courage to take my hand, look into my eyes, and say, *We fall down but we get up. / For we're people with a vision / who fall down and get up.*

MY EQUALITY COMPLEX?

The mindfulness bell rang as Thích Nhất Hạnh entered the dimly lit meditation hall. Nine hundred of us stood and bowed. Thankfully, my location allowed our eyes to briefly connect. I had arrived.

He walked slowly before the orchids, which were just as gentle and lovely as he was. We called him *Thây* (pronounced "tie"), Vietnamese for "teacher," and he called us "Buddhas-to-be." I stood, smiling, and considered it an honor to be in his presence. He placed his palms together and bowed to us.

The *sangha*, the Buddhist community, had gathered for a five-day retreat in upstate New York just as the autumn colors illuminated the hillside. I am certain none of us had read all of his hundred-plus books, but possibly between us all we had. Thích Nhất Hạnh had become a prominent world leader after being exiled from his homeland, Vietnam. During the Vietnam War he engaged in nonviolent civil disobedience, which inspired Martin Luther King Jr. to nominate him for a Nobel Peace Prize. Thây's commitment to peace and human rights became known as "engaged Buddhism."

As we returned to the lotus position, a young Buddhist nun stood serenely before the microphone and shared some big ideas: "We free ourselves from the inferiority complex, the superiority complex, the equality complex." I understood the first two, but the third? I wrote these phrases in my journal as two dozen nuns and monks mingled with one another and began to sing. Together they chanted about nondualism and nondiscrimination. It was inspired. The evening progressed with singing and stories and laughter. Thây retired to his study as we stayed for the orientation.

That orientation planted a painful seed in me. A young monk sat in lotus position on the platform. He instructed us to quietly enter the meditation hall at 5:45 a.m., with women sitting on one side and men the other. My spine straightened. Did he ask us to separate by gender?

We were then asked to practice noble silence as we mindfully climbed onto the bus for the thirty-minute ride to our hotels. A woman made eye contact with me as we left the lobby of our hotel to go to our rooms. I do not remember how our conversation began but will never forget how it ended. I asked, "Is it custom for men to sit separate from women in morning meditation?"

Tears rolled down her face.

Our conversation was sparse but piercing. She whispered, "Why can't we just sit together? Why all the divisions?"

❖   ❖   ❖

I fell into a troubled sleep. I felt itchy but was not scratching at my skin. My conscience was scratching at my imagination, replaying some of the mindfulness trainings.

- Protect the sangha by taking a stand and practicing understanding.
- Speak truthfully and use loving speech.
- Practice compassionate listening and reconcile all conflicts, however small.
- Dwell happily in the present moment and transform difficult emotions.
- Deal with anger by looking with the eyes of compassion.
- Commit to finding ways, including personal contact, to be with those who suffer.

- Renounce narrowness by practicing deeply.
- Understand that knowledge is not changeless, absolute truth.
- Remain determined not to be bound by any practices, even Buddhist ones.

Out of this state of complexity emerged serenity and clarity. The Holiday Inn notepad was just the right size for me to write Thây a brief letter.

Saturday, October 3, 2009

Dear Thây:

Aware of the suffering cased by segregation, my intention is to practice Mindful Integration by sitting with my sisters. I am determined to use my peaceful presence to cultivate equality for all.

With loving respect (and in the name you gave me),

Creative Generosity of the Heart (Nate Walker)

I awoke at 4:45 a.m., boarded the bus, and watched the moonshine fall on changing leaves. As I entered the meditation hall, a nun bowed to me. I handed her the note addressed to Thây. She smiled, bowed, and whispered, "I will give it to him." I bowed and placed my meditation cushion and blanket on the left side of the hall. Intending not only to communicate with Thây but also to assure the women sitting around me that my presence was not a threat to their safety, I gently distributed seven copies of my note to them, and then breathed into lotus position with eyes closed.

The sun rose. Chanting filled the hall. I was at peace.

After the final bell, as we silently walked toward the breakfast tents, a hand touched my shoulder. A woman I did not know looked at my nametag, and her eyes were bright. She bowed and mouthed, "Thank you." I bowed. We smiled.

❖ ❖ ❖

After mindful eating, walking, and working, the afternoon was open for mindful talking. We gathered in optional clusters of twenty or so dharma groups facilitated by monks and nuns. I was in the one that welcomed gay, lesbian, bisexual, and transgender people. I came to feel close to them and felt comfortable enough to share my note.

Some responded with gratitude, others with anger at gender separation, others with perplexity at the assumption of heterosexuality. We spoke of gender as a social construct, an illusion. We made distinctions between compelled segregation, as in the meditation, and the elective affinity sessions, as in the dharma groups. Others looked me in the eye and sincerely expressed concern about my "equality complex," which was difficult to hear. Regardless, we created for one another a place where deep listening and loving speech could occur. We all left enriched by one another's perspectives, one another's presence.

Meanwhile, I later learned, that other dharma groups were discussing the same subject. Some read aloud my letter to Thây, others had written their own. Some made the commitment to not separate from their families but to sit together as one.

However, the "dharma police," as one person put it, were in full force the next morning. At one point they were quite hostile. The women greeting us made clear that we were to separate by gender. I bowed and handed them my journal, in which a copy of the letter was scribed. It was quickly dismissed, but no one prevented me from accepting one woman's invitation to sit next to her.

❖ ❖ ❖

I later shared this story with a friend, who said, "Leave it to Nate to have to protest at a Buddhist retreat."

I could not help but laugh. After all, humor can often reveal truth.

❖ ❖ ❖

Days fell into one another. The silence touched a core part of my being. I took lovely walks. The people exuded kindness and the grounds were full of colors. Breathing became such a joy.

On the last day, in the last hours of the retreat, just before our buses left for the train, we were invited to a question-and-answer period with Thích Nhất Hạnh. I had crafted and then recrafted my question for Thây, genuinely interested in his response.

The session began with the children. One boy asked why he shaved his head. Thây replied, "To save money on shampoo." Another child asked if she could have a hug. His body-microphone amplified his simple "Yes" as he opened his arms. Then the children were invited to go and play as the adults were invited forward to ask questions of the Zen master. We were invited to listen to the mindfulness bell and out of the deep silence discern when to speak, allowing space between people, without feeling a need to rush the process.

Unfortunately, my bus was scheduled to be the first to depart, requiring me to leave early so I took the initiative to ask the second question. I sat in the empty chair and listened to the ringing of the bell. My eyes again connected with his, then fell to the page I was holding.

"Thây, my question is related to the request that women and men separate during morning meditation." I was only subtly aware of the nine hundred practitioners listening. "I contemplated this practice, listened to the suffering it caused my friends, and made the decision to practice nondualism and nondiscrimination by writing you the following two-sentence letter."

I read aloud the note with the intention not only of giving him the context of my question but of explaining to the sangha my previous communication with him.

I looked up to see him staring into the sea of people and said, "I reflected upon whether this practice derived from my equality complex." The sangha laughed. Thây smiled. I went on to read a second letter I had composed to him, explaining my understanding of the term: the belief in the illusion that we are separate from one another and therefore only happy when there is equality—delaying our happiness is a way to give more power to those we perceive as causing us suffering.

"I've meditated on this term and found it to be helpful when identifying how, in the name of openness, we become closed-minded. Yet it can be a harmful term when it's used to dismiss even the most insightful forms of equality," my letter went on. "My intention in practicing mindful integration is simple: to choose not to water the seeds passed on to me by my culture, my religion, and cultivated by many cultures, many religions throughout human history—the seeds of gender superiority.

"I know that whether or not we sit on separate sides during meditation, we are still equal. I am also aware that my country's history teaches me that separate-but-equal is still segregation.

"Thây, it felt so good this weekend, so good not to water these deeply rooted customs. It felt so good to be thanked by many women and many men for practicing mindful integration.

"In this context, I ask the following question with loving respect." I looked at my teacher and asked, "Sometime this next year, when lay and monastic practitioners gather during one morning meditation . . . will you invite us all to practice mindful integration?" The letter was signed with "Love, Nate" and my mailing address.

I bowed.

His response was unexpected in many ways. He first reached out his hand. I offered the hand-scribed letter but, with energy, he took the microphone instead. I thought he no longer wanted me to speak. I was wrong; he wanted another to have the microphone to answer the question.

He passed the microphone to the familiar young nun who was kneeling next to him. When Thây offered the microphone she shook her head and conveyed that she did not want to speak. Thây then gestured to the eldest nun, his meditation partner of fifty years, Sister Chân Không, who was sitting in the front row.

She placed her hands on the floor and crawled forward on all fours. Literally. When she reached a place beside the young nun, she arranged herself in lotus position. These nonverbal movements showed me that women were still treated as inferior to men.

Usually quite eloquent, Sister Chân Không stumbled in her efforts to describe Vietnamese culture. She told the story of a teenage girl whose father would no longer hug her because she had grown breasts. She consoled the daughter, listened to her pain, and helped her understand the importance of separating from men. She described it as a natural part of human behavior.

I remember lending her my attention while she spoke, and how her words sparked a smile in my eyes. She returned the respect. It was lovely to connect with her. She went on to explain that it is not discrimination to separate men and women in meditation: "That is wrong thinking," she said, smiling.

I bowed to her. I do not remember if she crawled or scooted back to her seat, I just know she did not stand.

The young nun returned the handheld microphone to Thây and he too explained that this practice was not segregation. He started by saying, "Ask any woman and she will tell you she likes to be with other women." He explained that in Plum Village, the spiritual community he founded in France, nuns live together and monks live together. They like to be together. It is not segregation. When there are more women than men in meditation, "the women sit behind the men," he said. He meant that even though this is the custom, a practice upheld by meditation-hall ushers, it is not dogmatically implemented on in all situations.

Thây described the suffering that comes from the inferiority complex, a wrong perception that comes from a lack of self-esteem. He talked about the superiority complex, "a disease" that comes from thinking that one is better than others. The equality complex is also a disease, he said, one that comes from thinking there is separation to begin with. "To think that this is segregation," he said, "is a kind of disease derived from wrong perceptions."

"There is a way out of this suffering," he proclaimed. "Look deeply into the nature of no-self. In Buddhism there is no self to separate. Know this and you will be free."

He bowed. I bowed. I walked slowly to my cushion, trying to breathe naturally. One woman touched my shin and bowed to me. I returned the gratitude. I walked away and boarded the bus.

❖ ❖ ❖

The sting of having my thinking labeled "diseased" lasted for about twenty-five minutes. This was most surprising. In the past, this kind of event would have left me feeling troubled for many moons. I had, after all, long since mastered the art of holding grudges. And yet it was the practice of mindfulness that set me free.

I began to see Thây as a continuation. Continuation is a Buddhist concept that explains that there is no birth, no death. We are a continuation of our ancestors, and our words and deeds continue past the time our body returns to the earth. I began to see Thây as a continuation of his teachers. He is, after all, the forty-second patriarch of the Lâm Té school of Zen Buddhism.

I began to see my experience at this retreat as an intercultural encounter between a Vietnamese and an American; an intergenerational encounter between an eighty-three-year-old and a thirty-three-year-old; and an interreligious encounter between a Zen master and a Unitarian Universalist minister. I began to see him as simply human. I was neither romanticizing him nor demonizing him.

I began to see myself, too, as simply human. I was, after all, the seventeenth settled minister of the historic First Unitarian Church of Philadelphia, established in 1796. The only female settled minister in its history was my colleague, Holly Horn, who served as co-minister with her husband. My ministry is a continuation of the same patriarchal system of which we are all a part. In this way, there is no separation between Thây and me. We are both continuations of all who came before, and our words and our deeds serve as continuations to our collective future. The questions remain:

How do we imagine the legacy on which our leadership rests, and how will our words and deeds heal the suffering ingrained in this continuation?

I hope to some day offer Thây a cup of tea so we can discuss another question. I would like to ask him how the recognition of no-self is spiritually achieved when the act of separating by gender draws attention to something that distinguishes us from others.

My question is intended to help me go deeper into the practice of mindfully applying the moral imagination. I began to see the situation through the eyes of the Vietnamese Zen Buddhists, through their worldview, which was constructed in a certain time and place and by a particular belief system.

Although questions still engage my consciousness, my appreciation for Thây became the balm that soothed the initial sting. There was something healing about Thây's human response. His insights about equality and no-self are certainly profound. However, I do not agree with their application in this context. I say this having spent many moons observing segregation in religious rituals.

Because I am a Unitarian Universalist, my faith journey has been informed by many spiritual practices that separate men from women. They are found in some Hindu temples and Sikh gurdwaras, in Mormon temples, in some Jewish synagogues and Muslim mosques, and in some Catholic rituals. In Transylvania, even Unitarians separate men from women in worship. These observations helped me understand that this particular meditation session was not an isolated practice in one particular sect of one world religion. My circle of compassion was expanded by my direct experience with the affirmation of gender separation by many world religions and by many cultures. I came to understand that gender separation is a deep-planted seed that can grow to bear fruits of spiritual, nonmaterial, separation.

I experience the freedom that comes of transcending the complexes that cloud my perceptions. I seek not to dominate but to co-exist. I seek not to diminish but to cultivate self-worth. I seek not to separate but to mindfully integrate. These intentions are made possible because of my experiment with the moral imagination, which allowed me to be a witness to a woman's pain. Her tears—which derived from feeling oppressed by systems of patriarchy, not an innate sense of inferiority—inspired me to practice mindfully and imagine myself to be at one with all who suffer.

May suffering, in any form, inspire us all to do likewise.

A LETTER TO MY MURDERER

K nit knew. Knit is a very smart kitty who knew exactly when to cuddle me. When a sadness would surface in me, or when he sensed that I was troubled, Knit would bury his roly-poly physique between my arm and ribs. Soon enough we would be involved in an interspecies cuddle-fest.

I had to shoo him away in order to complete my task: setting up the digital camera to record a pastoral message to the members of our congregation in Philadelphia. I had been their minister for a year and they had become accustomed to my use of technology. I pressed the red button, only to find Knit jumping into my lap. I was too emotionally drained to decline his invitation.

I looked into the camera and said, "Say hello. Say hello, Knit. Hi, church family. This is Reverend Nate. I'm here with my co-host, Kit Kat. He also goes by the name Knit and he's quite a cuddlebug." I continued to pet him; he occasionally looked into the camera as I conveyed some troubling news to my congregation.

That Sunday, July 27, 2008, a man had walked into the sanctuary of one of our sister congregations in Knoxville, Tennessee, opened a guitar case, pulled out a 12-gauge shotgun, and opened fire while children from two congregations were performing a musical. He wounded seven and killed one member of the Tennessee Valley Unitarian Universalist Church, Greg McKendry, and one member of the Westside Unitarian Universalist Church, Linda Kraeger.

I paused in my explanation of the event to say, "I've been cud-dling with Knit because the sadness is overwhelming. I'm sure you've been sad, too." I said that I was comforted by knowing that my dear colleagues were there, responding to the trauma. I was very proud of how our larger Unitarian Universalist family was coming together to tend to one another and to receive the care of so many other religious and secular groups. The outpouring of support from around the country was simply wondrous.

I used the second half of the video to prepare members for our service on Sunday, when we would not only mourn but reflect on a few questions. I asked, "How would you respond to such an event? As you know, this last fall we reflected in a worship service on the killings that occurred in an Amish schoolhouse not far from our community. We reflected on the fact that last November a shooting occurred just two blocks from our church after a board meeting.

"What is it about the violence in our communities? As you may know, Tennessee has the death penalty. I'm wondering, will the man who came into our sister congregation's sanctuary and killed two members of our family be placed on death row? Will Unitarian Universalists affirm capital punishment?"

I closed the video by inviting everyone to continue to research the events and to come to service on Sunday so we could be togeth-er as a family. I expressed my gratitude for being with this beautiful animal companion and expressed my love for those receiving my pastoral message.

❖   ❖   ❖

That night, I filled my journal with sketches and questions. I be-gan to experiment with the moral imagination by picturing myself as one who was murdered. I thought, if only we could turn back the clocks and ask Greg McKendry and Linda Kraeger what they would want.

This exercise reminded me of my conversations with those who were drafting their wills and determining their end-of-life care. Advance directives tell doctors about the kind of care we wish to have if we are, for example, in a coma and unable to make medical decisions. They not only allow doctors to know our wishes but also are helpful to our families, telling them what to do in times of crisis.

I began to doodle, recalling caring a few weeks earlier for a family in which a grandmother had left an advance directive. It informed the doctors that she was not to be kept alive by machines, should her heart stop or if she could no longer breathe. The term used in an advance directive to instruct this is DNR, Do Not Resuscitate; another term used in the field is AND, Allow Natural Death. It amazed me that there is a system that honors the wishes of the incapacitated and dying. I began to ask myself, what if we were to craft advance directives to address capital punishment?

Would Greg and Linda want their murderer to be killed by the state? If they had written their own form of advance directives, letters to their murderer, what would they say? What would they want their murderer to know? What statements would they make about his crime, and what kind of punishment would they affirm? Could such a statement make a difference, even if this idea has not yet been legally tested?

❖ ❖ ❖

It took five weeks to prepare myself emotionally to write my own letter. I intended to be disciplined and actually carry out this experiment.

I asked myself additional questions before doing so. Would the state take into consideration my wishes, the wishes of the one murdered? What comfort could such a letter bring to my family? What comfort could it offer to the murderer's family? Would it, could it, make any difference? If so, to whom?

I began by writing, "In the following letter, 'Mr. Atkisson' is the name given to my fictitious murderer. My words serve as an advance directive, informing my loved ones and the state of my dying wish. It does so by speaking directly to the one who may take my life. It is designed to be a personal statement of conscience to be used in any court of law."

Sunday, July 27, 2008

Dear Mr. Atkisson,

If you are reading this letter then it means you have taken my life. I am dead. You are alive.

I write this letter without awareness of your motives for killing —nor is it known to me the events in your own life that contributed to your actions. I do know, however, that my family must be in excruciating pain. I imagine my loved ones, my friends, my community weeping and cursing your name. They are probably asking "Why, why did you kill him?" It is likely they want to kill you with their bare hands. You have stripped me of my inherent worth and dignity, and they may want revenge.

We may not ever know why you killed me, but this much is true: You must repent. You must confess. You must make amends and sincerely and deeply apologize to my family. It is only right. Then you must receive your punishment.

Thankfully, we live in a justice-seeking nation and therefore you will be granted a fair trial and, if found guilty, will face severe repercussions. I cannot predict which jurisdiction your trial will be held in, nor what state and federal laws will be in place. I can, however, say that my trust lies in the system.

I believe it is right for the state to do anything in its power to remove you from society, so that you will not harm another living being. I believe it is right for the state to do anything in its power to make a bold statement to the world that whoever takes life will receive death.

I believe it is just for you to receive capital punishment because no one who takes life is worthy of living. I believe we must save society from murderers like you and therefore we must do God's work by sentencing you to death.

My dying wish is that whatever pain you may have caused me, you yourself experience. My dying wish is that my family members can, if they desire, be present for your execution. Your death will comfort them because they will be able to see with their own eyes that you are no longer in the world. In fact, your execution should be made public so that all who suffered, all who seek justice, can know that the state lawfully played its part in protecting us all. After your death, you will receive ultimate punishment. For only God will have the final judgment on your soul. I find comfort knowing that your soul will be damned and mine will be made whole.

I wonder if you ever knew love. . . . I wonder if there will be . . . I wonder. . . . Will this letter . . . the one composed to you now . . . will it ever have my signature?

Give me the strength to sign this letter—give me the strength to write another . . .

Sunday, July 27, 2008

Dear Mr. Atkisson,

If you are reading this letter then it means you have taken my life.

I am dead. You are alive.

You have received a fair trial and were found guilty. The state will inevitably choose an appropriate punishment for you; it is not mine to affirm or deny its decision. My faith lies in the system. I know those in power will do what is right.

I am but the dead—a voiceless victim of the past because you robbed me of my future. I am but the dead—a veiled memory of the past whose life will live on in the memories of my loved ones. I want to write to them and tell them how much they are loved. I learned from them patience and kindness. I learned from them honesty and gratitude. I learned from them to accept whatever comes. I accept the fact that you are now alive. I am dead. There is nothing left to do. I have no voice.

I am powerless to affect your actions or those of a system that will chart its own course. Fate will decide what happens. It is not mine to say.

It is not my responsibility to do anything. It is not my responsibility to even be writing this letter. Why give any attention to the one who stripped away my dignity? You do not even deserve to hear from me. Why bother? It's not like anything said here will matter anyway . . . or will it?

Sunday, July 27, 2008

Dear Mr. Atkisson,

If you are reading this letter then it means you have taken my life.

I am dead. You are alive.

I may be dead, but my life continues through the memories of my loved ones. My life continues through the legacy of these words. I am aware of my power. I am aware of my responsibility. I am aware that my words, my imagination, may determine your fate.

When I think of your future, the writings of my spiritual guides come to mind. I hear my teacher Thích Nhất Hạnh say, "I am determined not to kill, not to let others kill, and not to support any act of killing in the world, in my thinking, and in my way of life." I hear Gandhi say, "An eye for an eye makes the whole world blind." I hear Jesus say to the crowd who are about to stone a woman, "Let those without sin cast the first stone."

I am but one human life. I am a man who has made many mistakes, a man who has hurt many. I am not without sin. I have certainly been blinded by rage. Who is to say whether or not I would one day feel justified to kill? I suppose this letter puts me in such a situation.

I have the power to craft an advance directive to determine my end-of-life wishes—can I use this same method now to ask the state to take your life? If so, I could exercise the power to use my imagination to make your death my dying wish, which I don't want. My loved ones have the power to seek revenge in the name of justice by asking the state to sentence you to death; but they know true justice cannot be achieved through violence.

Martin Luther King Jr. said, "Through violence you may murder a murderer, but you can't murder murder. Through violence you may murder a hater, but you can't murder hate. Darkness cannot put out darkness. Only light can do that."

Where is the light in these dark days? Where is the light found in the belly of my family's grief? I imagine my loved ones experiencing excruciating pain, knowing that their Natie has been killed. Yet their suffering must pale in comparison to the pain your loved ones must be feeling, knowing that you have killed me.

I believe allowing you to live will be the most just punishment. Death is easy. Life—life is hard.

My dying wish is that you live.

You must come to live with yourself. You must live with the past. You must come to live with your sentence.

My hope is that the prosecutor or district attorney will not propose capital punishment as a result of my homicide. I hope you will receive a fair trial and that the judge and jury will look favorably on my words and pass a sentence in accordance with my wishes. If not, my hope is that the governor will grant you clemency, and pardon you from death row.

In no way should my statement be read to say you should go unpunished. You should be disciplined. But how?

I wish for you to be immediately removed from society. I wish that you may have time alone to sit with your thoughts, aware of the power of your moral imagination. As a Hindu prophet once said, "When we sow our thoughts, we reap our language; when we sow our language, we reap our actions; when we sow our actions, we reap our habits; when we sow our habits, we reap our character; when we sow our character, we reap our destiny."

I wish for you to have time with others to help process your thoughts, aware that your actions have shaped your destiny and mine. I wish for adequate resources to be given to you to aid in your eventual rehabilitation. In that time, my hope is that you will be given the responsibility to preserve life.

I want you to be sentenced to grow a garden. I want you to name your plants after those in history who have sought to preserve life—give each plant a human name, and teach others about the significance of the names. Be disciplined about caring for life. My hope is that you will do everything in your power to keep them alive. In time, those aiding in your rehabilitation may deem you ready to care for another being.

When you are ready, my wish is that you be entrusted with caring for a kitty cat. Please name him Nate. I want you to take care of your new animal companion. Treat him with dignity, just as you seek to preserve your own. Discipline him with care, just as you discipline yourself by practicing self-care.

I believe in you. I believe in the power of your imagination to reform yourself.

You may have taken my life; you may have stripped me of my dignity; you may have harmed my loved ones beyond belief; but know that the cycle of violence will not ease their pain, nor will it bring me back to life. My life will only continue if you preserve the essence of my memory.

Here lies your charge: Use your power to preserve my memory; use your power to preserve your dignity; use your power to preserve life.

I close with some questions for you: What will you do with your new life? What purpose will come from these events? What vision will you craft for yourself? What thoughts will dominate your mind?

Just as these questions are asked of you, one question remains for me. Will this letter receive my signature?

❖ ❖ ❖

And for those reading these words, the question is not which letter will receive my signature, but what kind of letter will you include with your will?

A MINISTRY OF MEDIATION

placed two envelopes on the sanctuary chancel of the First Unitarian Church of Philadelphia as the service began. The children in the congregation helped me open them, one by one. The first held a piece of paper that read, "Imagine a house on fire. A baby is inside. Do you save the baby?"

"On three," I told everyone, "all who think the baby is worthy of being saved run over here and pretend to pull the baby from the fire." The cluster of kids and adults were poised. "Ready? One, two ... three!"

Naturally, everyone saved the baby. It was important to explain that this was just a game and that we do not want anyone to actually run into a burning building. I then asked a second grader, "Why did you want to save the baby?"

He responded, "Because the baby is a human person."

The congregation applauded. Then I read them the paper that was inside the second envelope.

"A house is on fire. Inside is a baby named Adolf Hitler. Who was Adolf Hitler? He was the chancellor of Germany in the 1930s and 1940s who led the Nazis to kill more than 6 million Jews, gay people, and Romani. Imagine that he is inside the burning house. On three, we have to determine who, if anyone, believes baby Hitler is worthy of being saved. Ready? One, two ... three!"

Two kids decided to save baby Hitler.

I went near them with the handheld microphone, but decided

to first ask the adults, "Why *didn't* you save baby Hitler?"

Everyone laughed while one woman replied, "Um. I couldn't decide if it was better for me to have him stay or drag him out to face the courts."

"Yes, it is a moral dilemma, isn't it?"

I turned to another adult. "And why didn't you save baby Hitler?"

She replied, "I knew that little man"—pointing to a third grader —"would be all on it."

Giving the microphone to him, I asked, "So why *did* you decide to save baby Hitler?"

He said, simply, "There is worth in every human being."

The congregation erupted in applause.

❖　❖　❖

After singing the children out of the sanctuary to do their own activities, we spent the rest of the service reflecting on the historic theology of Universalism and the first Principle of Unitarian Universalism: the inherent worth and dignity of every person. A worship associate explained, "Universalists believe that God is too good to damn; Universalists believe not in original sin but in universal salvation, that all will be reconciled by the love from which we are all born. We seek to emulate this universal love by affirming and promoting our first Principle, the inherent worth and dignity of every person, every being. Therefore, no matter who may be trapped in the burning building, Universalists teach us that everyone is worthy of being saved. But saved from what?"

This question set me up to mention Alfred Cole's charge: "to give them, not hell, but hope and courage." I said, "Aware that hell is not a place but a state of being, aware that hell is what we make for one another here and now, we must have the courage to save ourselves from the hell that we create, especially when we are responsible for fueling the fire of fear and judgment."

I began my talk by explaining that fear and judgment are the elements that form the *discriminatory mind*, a way of thinking that is quick to condemn, because at its root it is poised to defend itself by any means necessary. I reminded the congregation of the different ways of otherizing described by Robert Schreiter, especially demonizing, generalizing, and vaporizing. Otherizing is made possible when a mind that is quick to judge meets a heart that is fraught with fear. And I explained to them the firestorm that our church had endured just a few days before.

❖ ❖ ❖

The story began with a viral email: a press release from a group called Anti-Racist Action. It declared that the First Unitarian Church of Philadelphia was about to "play host to One Life Crew, a racist, homophobic, hardcore band," and that there was no doubt that the Keystone State Skinheads, a Pennsylvania white-power group, would be "attending the show in force." "Reverend Nate Walker," it added, "is fully aware of this show," but "stated that the church would not 'censor its tenants.'" And it asked its readers to call my cell phone and to email the nine congregational leaders, whose contact information it also listed, to persuade them to "shut down the show."

The organization sent the email to ministers and social justice leaders in countless congregations throughout the country; to the trustees of the Unitarian Universalist Association, our national organization and the trustees of the district in which my congregation was located; to the executive committee of the Unitarian Universalist Ministers Association; and to countless staff and anti-oppression leaders throughout our denomination.

Within forty-eight hours, I received calls from the Philadelphia and Pennsylvania State Commissions on Human Relations, the American Jewish Committee, the Anti-Defamation League, and two detectives from Homeland Security. Additionally, countless Unitarian Universalist lay people and ministers from Pennsylvania, New Jersey, New York, Montana, California, Texas, Oregon, and Michigan, as well as elsewhere, emailed and called me to say, as one person put it, "the image of the entire denomination was at stake." Another person told me, "UUs who are Jewish and gay and people of color and Latina/Latino feel that if you host this concert you rob them of the promise of a safe and welcoming place." A ministerial colleague wrote, "Censorship is merely a façade when you profit from hate speech."

All of these emails arrived on the same day that representatives of my congregation testified in City Hall in opposition to a developer's plans to build a high-rise that would eclipse our Center City church. In that context, another colleague wrote, "How can you fear the loss of sunlight from a neighboring building when you've cast a shadow on yourself?"

These are but a few examples of how within two days our church caught on fire. We extinguished the blaze by integrating the healing power of direct communication; by engaging the healing power of study; and by using the healing power of the moral imagination as a spiritual discipline.

❖ ❖ ❖

Several months before the firestorm, the church staff and trustees had been contacted about this concert by members of Anti-Racist Action and One People's Project, two groups that monitor the behavior of neo-Nazis through a decentralized network of militant anti-fascists and anti-racists. We had deep sympathy for their mission, but concerns about the means by which they pursued it. Over those months we confirmed that our tenant, R5 Productions, had not scheduled One Life Crew to perform there. A few days before the press release went out, we learned that a third party had booked the space on the band's behalf and was advertising its concert there. We practiced direct communication by asking the band's promoter/manager about its lyrics and the history of the controversy surrounding it.

Meanwhile, we engaged in multiple pastoral conversations with members of Anti-Racist Action and One People's Project, who clearly had a long and violent history with the band and with those who they thought would be attending the concert. I learned that over twelve years before, fights had broken out at One Life Crew concerts, and since then both supporters and opponents of the band had been arrested on various charges. The feud had only gotten worse over the years. The church had become the locus of an anticipated showdown.

I explained to the leaders of Anti-Racist Action that we needed time to consult with R5 Productions, to speak with the band, and to discuss whether or not we had the legal authority to censor the activities of our tenants. I asked rhetorically, "Can we tell the daycare centers that lease the church what they can teach, or guest preachers what they can preach, or guest musicians what lyrics they can sing?" These words were used to make it look as if the church was "determined to host" a hate group, which the minister "refused to censor."

I continued to practice direct communication by responding to the controversy with a public pastoral letter, which, it can be argued, added more fuel to the fire. I began by educating the public about our ten-year relationship with R5 Productions, its practice of producing drug- and alcohol-free concerts, its excellent security and history of hiring off-duty police. I made clear that if skinheads were to attend and cause violence they would be dealt with immediately, just as anyone would who becomes a threat on church property.

I publicly invited Anti-Racist Action and the band to work with the church to create a public process to help the community talk about racism and homophobia. I did so because I believe that conflict is an opportunity for deeper intimacy. Intimacy is necessary to build trusting, authentic relationships. I made clear that through a ministry of mediation there would be two privately filmed events to later be published online. The first interview would be with members of Anti-Racist Action and the second would be with the band, at which I planned to ask the musicians about the differences between free speech and hate speech.

This anti-oppression philosophy is simple: Being in relationship heals racism and homophobia; refusing to be in relationship perpetuates fear and judgment. In other words, by demonizing people we have never met or know little about, we use our fear to justify their elimination; by treating them as non-individuals, we generalize them and justify not acknowledging their presence at all. But through relationships, we have the power to give them "not hell, but hope and courage." This is made possible when the moral imagination, put into action, brings together a punk band, skinheads, radical activists, and me, an openly gay minister who is in an interracial relationship with an immigrant.

I invited the community to join in this process—to witness against hate speech and to work with neighbors and area congregations to stand against oppression. I made it clear that we would do everything in our power to create a secure, safe, and healthy setting in which to engage with some of the most morally challenging issues of our time. I invited everyone to speak with me directly if they had advice, questions, or concerns.

Some leaders of my congregation rightfully questioned whether I could make such a public pastoral statement or whether, since I was not just a minister but also the church's executive director, it should have been vetted by congregational leaders, or even approved by the board. These are all healthy and important questions about process and decision-making and the timely matter of prophetic outreach.

Outside my church, most appreciated my willingness to engage in this urban ministry. Some were outraged by my choice not to use my power to immediately shut down the show. For me, it was critical to immediately engage in the spiritual discipline of study. This discipline is usually applied to learning scripture. In this context, I sought to study the conflict itself, as if it were a text that could reveal something about the human condition.

❖ ❖ ❖

Together, staff from the national Unitarian Universalist Association and the district, Unitarian Universalist ministers and leaders, and staff at First Unitarian continued to study the situation, its history, and its context. During this time we held a dozen conference calls in which we examined the lyrics of the band and spoke with local, state, and federal officials. We ended up with an incredible amount of data about every single individual involved in this conflict.

This gave me the necessary information to speak directly with the band and to welcome into my office one of the leaders of Keystone State Skinheads, who started the meeting by asking, "Reverend Nate, were you afraid to meet with me?"

I leaned in and said, "No, were you afraid to meet with me?"

We laughed, and he clarified that KSS had moved from being a "white power" group that was known for its violent attacks to being a "white pride" group that, he said, is nonviolent—although I had evidence to the contrary. He admitted that it maintains "white nationalist" views.

We spoke of his police record, the fact that he had been coming to concerts at the church for the last decade, and his deep concerns about multiculturalism and illegal immigration. We even had a respectful discussion of the complex issue of homosexuality. It was clear that we had different views on these topics, but that did not keep us from upholding each other's dignity.

At the end of our conversation, he expressed his respect for the church and said, "Thank you for not making me out to be a monster." Then he shook my hand and hugged me.

❖   ❖   ❖

I spoke with the band by phone the following morning and asked about their racist lyrics. They began to laugh. "What's so funny?" I asked. And they replied, "We have a Turkish singer, a Russian-Arab guitarist, and our drummer is Jewish." They explained that although they had been made out to be a hate group, in reality they were all in their late forties, with kids and full-time jobs, and they had put out an album twelve years earlier with lyrics that did not reflect their current beliefs.

I specifically asked them about one of their previously published songs that started with the singer screaming "Fag," followed by the sound of a machine gun. I asked them if it was referring to me personally. They backtracked, apologized, and told me they said those things to get a reaction from "those liberal fascists."

We had a long talk about how liberal fundamentalism is born when we who take pride in being open-minded close our minds— when we become what we set out against.

I explained that their lyrics and the sound of machine guns did not shock me. I then read to them a passage in the Christian New Testament that says homosexuals deserve death (Romans 1:26–32). I explained that whether such a message is in scripture or in punk lyrics, it is my responsibility to study the words and to understand their context, to not fall victim to an undisciplined mind. I explained that my commitment to observe without reacting motivated me to learn about the context in which they wrote those lyrics.

I asked if they understood the consequences of hate speech, and how it could be seen as inviting others to behave violently. I told them about the man who opened fire on our sister congregation in Knoxville, Tennessee, because he hated liberals and a church that welcomes gay people. I asked them if they intended to use such words to provoke others to do the same. We had a healthy discussion about the differences between free speech and hate speech.

I asked them why they wanted to perform at the church. They said, "Because *Rolling Stone* says your church is one of the top punk venues in the country." I then took the advice of my colleague Keith Kron and asked if they would be willing to donate the proceeds of the concert to the Human Rights Campaign and the Freedom to Marry fund. And then I invited them to participate in a public forum with me and to explain how their beliefs had evolved over the years.

They replied, "Man, we'd do anything for you, Reverend Nate, anything, but . . . the thing is, if we clear our name then people won't think we're crazy."

My eyes widened. I said, "That's the point!"

They explained that the more fear that people had about the band, the more popular they became. I then asked, "Well, then why, in the pursuit of fame, would you want to defame the church—the organization that would be viewed as giving a bullhorn to a racist and homophobic band?"

They said, "That's why we'll cancel the show. We'll cancel it," they said. "You have shown us respect, so we'll respect the church."

We ended the call. I then spoke to the third-party promoter, who had been an excellent communicator through the entire process. He, too, agreed to cancel the concert.

This experience led me to reflect upon the spiritual practice that formed this ministry of mediation: the willingness to experiment with the moral imagination, especially in the most trying of circumstances.

❖   ❖   ❖

We can intentionally use our imaginations to picture ourselves as the other. We can observe how misperceptions are born and how fear is fueled. We can imagine the pain that has built up over time among those who have been in conflict for more than a decade. We can imagine what it must be like to be groomed from childhood to be a skinhead. We can imagine what it must be like to be so fiercely committed to an anti-racist agenda that we see even the police, government, and churches as our enemies, because they often perpetuate systems of oppression. We can acknowledge the cliché that "hurt people hurt people."

To experiment with the moral imagination is to empathize, to sympathize, and to understand. And while understanding need not mean agreement, it is necessary in order to heal the poison found in a heart bound by fear and in a mind bound by judgments.

The discriminatory mind is healed when we imagine ourselves as the other, which leads me to reflect upon the nature of pride and to pose a final question.

❖   ❖   ❖

The day after the concert was canceled, leaders of the church joined me in a face-to-face conversation with the leaders of One People's Project and the Philadelphia chapter of Anti-Racist Action. They apologized for not having given us time to process information and for being so quick to condemn a church whose strategy differed from their own. They began to use their imagination to empathize with a church whose values are similar to their own.

Later, Anti-Racist Action put out a statement with a headline that read, "VICTORY: One Life Crew will not play in Philadelphia!" They felt proud that dozens and dozens of people had mounted a campaign against our church. The band and the promoter later told me they felt proud because they took the "high road." They respected the church and chose to cancel the concert. And then there's me, who proudly explains in this chapter the significance of a ministry of mediation. I suppose we could call this a win-win-win situation.

There's one thing that left members of our congregation feeling proud. Countless ministers and leaders of our denomination immediately and thoughtfully dropped everything and were poised to support the church's urban ministry. I received lovely phone messages, encouraging emails, and strategic advice that made this experiment possible. I had never before felt such a deep connection to an intricate sisterhood of congregations, a religious movement that is so intricately tied to a social justice movement. Numerous community officials and national leaders were committed to being a nonanxious presence—which we called "taking a NAP." Countless people who had been elected to serve the Unitarian Universalist Association, to serve its districts, and to serve the historic Philadelphia congregation treated me with the utmost respect and diligently worked together, and of that we can all be proud.

❖   ❖   ❖

Finally, this question: "A church is on fire. A minister, a punk band, some skinheads, and some anti-racist activists are all inside. Who do you save from the fire?"

Everyone.

Because we are all worthy of being saved from the fires, even the ones that we helped to create. We are saved through a ministry of mediation rooted in universal love. By using direct communication, study, and the moral imagination as spiritual disciplines, we can save one another from the judgmental mind and the fearful heart.

We are all merely babies. We are all growing and learning. We are all worthy of being saved from the fires of the discriminatory mind. We are saved from these fires when we individually and collectively use the moral imagination to preserve the worth and dignity of every person—without exception.

THE MONSANTO BEAST

will never forget the moment when the skinhead hugged me and said, "Thank you for not making me out to be a monster." His comment stilled me.

I could not help but think of this encounter a year later, when I received a series of threatening letters. One anonymous one had been sent from a New Hampshire post office. It was a single piece of paper, a photocopy of a pencil sketch of the face of a colossal beast. Its fangs dripped with blood and from its mouth protruded a stick figure with the label "Rev. Nate." Tattooed on the beast's forehead were eight letters: MONSANTO.

Monsanto, an agrochemical and agricultural biotechnology corporation, is often portrayed as a monster for its work with genetically modified foods. The person who drew the beast, and the dozen-plus other people who also sent aggressive remarks, were responding to a feature article in the Unitarian Universalist magazine *UU World* titled "Dinner with Monsanto," written by journalist Michelle Bates Deakin. In it, she described how our urban Philadelphia congregation had collectively practiced the moral imagination in engaging with Monsanto executives.

We launched the experiment in November 2009, when I delivered a sermon that was a public letter to Monsanto CEO Hugh Grant. In it, I asked him seven questions about his moral relationship with farmers, consumers, the media, universities, governments, creation, and his conscience. The letter closed with a request that we meet in public to discuss these questions. To my surprise, he agreed to have me meet privately with him and his executives at the company's headquarters in St. Louis. Two church trustees and I accepted, insisting we pay our own way.

What was supposed to be a two-hour meeting became four days of profound conversations with fourteen executives and members of the Monsanto board of directors. We toured the facilities and attended a shareholder meeting at which we met with representatives of the Interfaith Center on Corporate Responsibility. At the time, these representatives were religious leaders who use their power as shareholders to work for social change.

Our conversations with Monsanto executives centered on our church's invitation to Monsanto to take the lead in organizing an interfaith group of clergy and bioethicists to develop a twenty-first-century Hippocratic Oath for the field of biotechnology. We envisioned the oath as based on the principles of biomedical ethics, such as nonmaleficence (do no harm), beneficence (do good), and distributive justice (be fair). We proposed the name "The Grant Oath," hoping that Mr. Grant would help draft and sign it and that his employees and his corporate competitors would sign it as well.

We wanted to inspire Monsanto executives to imagine unveiling the Grant Oath, calling on all those who produce genetically modified foods to consider the possible harm that any pursuit of scientific advancement may have on people, animals, or the environment. We wanted Grant to imagine leaving an enduring legacy to humanity in the form of a code of ethics for the entire field of biotechnology:

I promise to use my expertise to help and not harm people, animals, and the environment. I promise to practice responsibly the ancient ethic of stewardship and the modern principle of sustainability by affirming distributive justice as a moral obligation to benefit the interdependent web of existence of which we are all a part.

The St. Louis dialogue was so successful that Monsanto executives flew to Philadelphia in July to meet with our church leaders and continue to discuss the proposed oath. But soon after the Philadelphia dialogue, the executive who served as our primary contact was abruptly laid off. This was just as chilling as when executives throughout the deliberations declined our request to participate in creating an oath because, as they routinely stated, they believed that Monsanto was already "doing no harm."

❖   ❖   ❖

Many know Monsanto as a chemical company, which it was for most of the twentieth century, but it has since become a multinational agricultural biotechnology corporation. It produces 90 percent of the world's genetically engineered seeds, including soy, corn, cotton, and most recently alfalfa. At the time of our meetings in 2009, its market value was $44 billion, and in that year it sold $7.3 billion worth of seeds and seed genes. Monsanto spent less than 10 percent of its research budget on chemicals, it claimed, and the rest was split evenly between conventional breeding and genetic engineering.

The company's conventional research focuses on developing hybrid seeds that are adapted to different types of soil and weather. Its genetic research focuses on transferring desirable traits from one plant species to another, using a soil bacterium to carry the relevant genes from the first species to the second. Desirable traits include such things as resistance to insects or to the herbicide in a weed killer, and greater yield per acre. In 2008, Monsanto announced a commitment to "double yield in its three core crops of corn, soybeans, and cotton by 2030" to "meet the needs [of a growing world population] for increased food, fiber, and energy while protecting the environment." Monsanto believes that, in a global system of farmers, governments, and organizations, it can play a part in ending world hunger.

This mission, however, is not exempt from controversy. Monsanto's work is not free from criticism, nor is it immune to the concerns of the organic industry and consumers. This is why we posed a wide range of complex questions to its executives.

For instance, we asked them about the drinking water in Anniston, Alabama, that was contaminated because, more than forty years ago, Monsanto dumped forty-five tons of PCB pollutants into an open-pit landfill. In 2003, Monsanto and its spin-off company, Solutia, agreed to pay a $700 million settlement because of this environmental damage. We also asked about its involvement in developing DDT and Agent Orange. We asked about the international studies that found the DNA of genetically modified crops in the milk, blood, liver, kidneys, and intestinal tissues of animals who were fed those crops. We asked about a letter sent by a group of influential scientists to the Environmental Protection Agency saying that Monsanto was preventing "university scientists from fully researching the effectiveness and environmental impact of the industry's genetically modified crops."

❖   ❖   ❖

Our questions were not our only tools. We applied three spiritual practices to our public advocacy: doubt, deep listening and loving speech, and the moral imagination.

We began by posing questions to one another about our beliefs and assumptions so that we could reflect on the authenticity of our words and our deeds. We were aware that doubt played a powerful role in our moral and intellectual growth. We considered doubt to be a seed we could water in all of us, which flowered in a three-word question: "Are you sure?" Throughout the process, I challenged myself to listen to this question, asking myself, "Nate, are you sure that your critiques of Monsanto are rooted in the most credible research? Nate, are you sure you are speaking with integrity?" I sought to water this seed of doubt not only to better my character but also to model for Monsanto executives how they could ask, "Are we sure? Are we sure we are doing everything in our power to do no harm, to do good, and to be just?" Over the year after members of my congregation and I started this conversation, I saw that both Monsanto employees and members of our church family revere the seed of doubt. It quieted us. The seed created for us a culture of deliberation rather than debate. It allowed us to build a relationship based on the mutual commitment to develop a culture of learning established on the second spiritual practice: deep listening and loving speech.

Going into the deliberations, we knew that language had power. Language could cause suffering or, if chosen mindfully and spoken truthfully, could inspire confidence and hope. In this way, we practiced compassionate listening and used words that sought not to demean one another but to inspire us to make meaning about complex matters. We believed that deep listening and loving speech need not devalue the strength or power of our concerns. This was not a saccharine practice that glossed over reality. It was a way to communicate effectively—to open up conversations rather than use words to slam ears shut. The practice of deep listening and loving speech fed our conscience rather than our aggression. We knew all too well how fear and anger could plague our thoughts, our words, and our actions, leading us to perceive a person, or in this case a company, as "the other." When we failed in that way, we gave ourselves permission to treat "the other" as a stranger to be feared or eliminated. We countered this destructive pattern of "otherizing" with a creative one, based on the third spiritual practice: the moral imagination.

Ralph Waldo Emerson said, "That which dominates our imaginations and our thoughts will determine our lives, our character." This wisdom inspired the way we sought to engage in global ministry: We worked to develop our moral imagination by picturing ourselves through the eyes of another. This prevented us from demonizing the leaders in the biotech industry, treating Monsanto as an organization to be feared. It also set a tone through which the executives could not romanticize their own efforts, treating Monsanto as a company that could do no wrong. Intellectual honesty became a hallmark of our deliberations. In this way, people who held both the organic and biotech worldviews engaged in a public dialogue by making a covenant based on the simple idea that there is no stranger. We lived this ethic by picturing ourselves in another's shoes and thereby intimately wove our imagination with the practice of deep listening and loving speech and, most importantly, with the spiritual practice of doubt, leading us all to ask simply, "Are we sure?"

❖   ❖   ❖

Our encounters with Monsanto reinforced for me the urgency of using the moral imagination as an everyday spiritual practice. We and the Monsanto executives could have spent our time together demeaning and demoralizing one another; instead, we used it to make meaning with one another about the ethical issues of our time. I was transformed by these deliberations, and I have reasons to believe the participants were, too—both the fourteen executives and the members of my religious community.

Although Monsanto was the subject of our public inquiries, the primary focus of this grand experiment was always my church members' moral and intellectual development. We failed to produce a concrete result, such as an oath, but we did gain a non-material reward, one that shaped our character as individuals and as a community. This developmental process took more than a year.

In June 2009, the delegates to General Assembly, the Unitarian Universalist Association's annual national meeting, voted to make "ethical eating" a denominational study item—in which local congregations would offer courses and worship services on the topic. I facilitated an adult religious education class on the issue. That was when we first began to formulate the questions I ultimately posed to Hugh Grant in my sermon that November. Congregants were ecstatic when we were invited to St. Louis. They spent hours preparing those of us who would travel to the Monsanto headquarters in January. They were thrilled to hear about the successful outcomes of those dialogue sessions and were even more excited to prepare themselves to welcome Monsanto executives when they would visit us in Philadelphia in July. And they extended their own conversation by choosing "food justice" as the church's 2011–12 social justice theme; we would spend the year further examining issues of food security and ethical eating. Each of these events contributed to a culture of justice, rooted in the practice of the moral imagination.

These exchanges were radically different from those that had occurred years earlier, when members of the social justice ministry team were often embroiled in arguments over not supporting one another's causes. Those team members could also be found at town hall meetings publicly shaming those they perceived as their oppressors. Church leaders spent many moons fueling the fires of liberal fundamentalism. And yet, throughout the yearlong dialogue with Monsanto, I witnessed these same people—the ones who had vociferously screamed "PEACE!" at peace rallies—being truly peaceful, principled, and competent.

I saw members of my community be intellectually honest, ethically engaged, compassionate, and, most of all, effective communicators. They learned to articulate what they opposed by posing nonviolent questions. Doing this required them to be curious rather than furious. It gave everyone access to power that no liberal fundamentalist would ever have. The deliberation sessions taught my parishioners to release all notions of duality, to no longer see themselves as the heroes and those who disagreed with them as the villains. They learned to articulate not only what they were against, but also what they were for. Rather than storming the Monsanto castle, they learned to knock on the door and deliver an invitation—an invitation to collaborate in drafting an oath. They found this approach much more effective than demands or threats.

They learned to listen, to be open, and ultimately to understand that the Monsanto executives they spoke with were motivated not by malice but by altruism. They were shocked when one said that she lay awake at night worrying that the organic industry would not produce enough food to feed the growing population. They began to see that Monsanto executives felt that they were doing good, and they appreciated that the executives acknowledged the company's previous harmful acts. Many of them understood and appreciated the executives' perspectives but ultimately disagreed with Monsanto's corporate worldview and approach.

These moments were the most fulfilling experiences in my career as a minister and educator. I watched my community take an intellectually sophisticated approach to justice-making. This process began by recognizing that understanding is a necessary component of social justice and that it does not necessarily imply agreement. I saw members of my community learn to differentiate themselves from others without making others out to be monsters. They were able to preserve the inherent worth and dignity of every person while simultaneously and judiciously rejecting the immoral behavior of others and themselves.

Unfortunately, the Monsanto dialogue sessions, as reported in *UU World*, were so threatening to liberal fundamentalists outside our congregation that they characterized me as a lone patsy being consumed by the Monsanto beast. The very thought of dialoguing with leaders of Monsanto was repulsive to these critics, in the same way that some people say, "We don't negotiate with terrorists." Their harsh comments and threatening letters, such as the drawing of me being consumed by the Monsanto beast, illustrate a deficit in their moral imagination.

This was the same deficit I experienced when I demeaned a woman in pearls at a lecture and when I dehumanized my biological father. To a different degree, it was the same deficit in morality that bred apartheid in South Africa and genocide in Rwanda. It was the lack of a moral imagination in leaders of the U.S. government that enabled them to justify using Agent Orange in Vietnam and denying medical treatment to people infected with HIV. It was the same moral deficit that enabled religious leaders to justify causing physical or legal harm to sexual minorities or characterizing systematic gender segregation as benign. It was the same moral deficit that led protesters to demand that I not negotiate with murderers, skinheads, or Monsanto executives.

I disagree. I have come to witness the power of skillful engagement with the moral issues of our time. Each of these disputes, regardless of the stakes, challenged members of my religious community to use the moral imagination as an everyday spiritual practice. Some of these encounters engulfed our community in fierce disputes, while others we merely watched from across the arc of the world. Some were personal squabbles over petty matters, such as a theater seat, and others were global issues of life and death. Regardless of the potency or proximity of the disputes, each required that we practice, over and over, the lessons that we thought we had already learned. Our congregation became a training ground, and each conflict became an experiment, an opportunity to develop our morality and our mind. These experiments gave us a newfound purpose for our gatherings week after week.

As a community, we learned that the moral imagination is not something you acquire once and then eternally possess. We may have the capacity to apply it in one situation and fail to do so in the next. In fact, although this book is a mostly chronological account, my humiliation of the woman in pearls, described in the first chapter, was actually the most recent event. Even after skillfully engaging in dialogue with a Zen master, skinheads, and leaders at Monsanto, I erupted over someone taking my partner's theater seat. How petty. In other words, even after spending years experimenting with the moral imagination, I regressed under stress.

This is why the moral imagination must be an everyday practice, a competency that is cultivated with every thought, every action. Ultimately, the experiments that I have recounted dared us all to individually and collectively use our moral imaginations to achieve something that none of us would have been able to do alone. This is how I came to know that this practice is not simply an individual discipline but a communal one.